First World War
and Army of Occupation
War Diary
France, Belgium and Germany

48 DIVISION
Divisional Troops
Royal Army Medical Corps
1/1 South Midland Field Ambulance
30 March 1915 - 31 October 1917

WO95/2752/1

The Naval & Military Press Ltd
www.nmarchive.com
Published in association with The National Archives

Published by

The Naval & Military Press Ltd

Unit 10 Ridgewood Industrial Park,

Uckfield, East Sussex,

TN22 5QE England

Tel: +44 (0) 1825 749494

www.naval-military-press.com

www.nmarchive.com

This diary has been reprinted in facsimile from the original. Any imperfections are inevitably reproduced and the quality may fall short of modern type and cartographic standards.

Contents

Document type	Place/Title	Date From	Date To
Heading	WO95/2752/1 1/1 South Midland Field Ambulance		
Heading	48th Division 1-1st Sth Mid'd Fld Amb Apr 1915-1917 Oct From 67 Div		
Heading	1/1st S.M. Field Ambulance Vol I		
War Diary	Harve	30/03/1915	30/03/1915
War Diary	Cassel	01/04/1915	01/04/1915
War Diary	Oudizeele	01/04/1915	04/04/1915
War Diary	Bailleul	05/04/1915	10/04/1915
War Diary	Armentieres	11/04/1915	16/04/1915
War Diary	Romarin	17/04/1915	30/04/1915
Heading	48th Div 1st S.M. Field Ambulance Vol II		
War Diary	Romarin	01/05/1915	04/05/1915
War Diary	Pont De Nieppe	05/05/1915	31/05/1915
Miscellaneous	Appendix I		
Heading	48th Division War Diary 1st South Midland Field Ambulance Vol III		
War Diary	Pont De Nieppe	01/06/1915	25/06/1915
War Diary	Vieux Berquin	26/06/1915	26/06/1915
War Diary	Gonnehem	27/06/1915	27/06/1915
War Diary	Allouagne	28/06/1915	30/06/1915
Heading	48th Division 1st S.M. Field Ambulance Vol IV		
War Diary	Allouagne	01/07/1915	15/07/1915
War Diary	Ames	16/07/1915	21/07/1915
War Diary	Sarton	22/07/1915	31/07/1915
Heading	48th Division 1st S.M. Field Ambulance Vol V From 1st To 31st Aug 1915		
War Diary	Sarton	01/08/1915	06/08/1915
War Diary	Arqueves	07/08/1915	09/08/1915
War Diary	Sarton	06/08/1915	06/08/1915
War Diary	Arqueves	07/08/1915	31/08/1915
Heading	48th Division 1/1st S.M. Field Ambulance Vol VI Sept 15		
War Diary	Arqueves	01/09/1915	30/09/1915
Heading	48th Division 1/1 S.M Fd Amb Oct 15 Vol VII		
War Diary	Arqueves	01/10/1915	31/12/1915
Heading	1st S.M Fd Amb Vol IX		
Heading	1/1 S.M Fd Amb Vol X & XIII Jan 1916		
War Diary	Arqueves	01/01/1916	31/01/1916
Heading	48th Division 1/1 S.M. Field Ambulance Feb 1916		
Heading	1/1 SM Fd Amb Feb Vol XI		
War Diary	Arqueves	01/02/1916	04/02/1916
War Diary	Bertrancourt	05/02/1916	29/02/1916
Heading	48th Div 1/1 S.M Field Ambulance March 1916		
War Diary	Bertrancourt	01/03/1916	04/03/1916
War Diary	Bus	05/03/1916	31/03/1916
Heading	48th Div 1/1st S. Midland F Amb. April 1916		
War Diary	Souastre	01/04/1916	30/04/1916
Heading	48th Div 1st S. Mid. F. Amb. May 1916		
War Diary	Souastre	01/05/1916	04/05/1916
War Diary	Beauval	05/05/1916	31/05/1916

Heading	48th Division 1/1 S.M Field Ambulance June 1916		
War Diary	Beauval	01/06/1916	09/06/1916
War Diary	Hem	10/06/1916	16/06/1916
War Diary	Arqueves	16/06/1916	30/06/1916
Heading	48th Div 1/1st South Mid Field Amb.		
War Diary	Arqueves	01/07/1916	07/07/1916
War Diary	Thievres	08/07/1916	14/07/1916
War Diary	Contay	15/07/1916	15/07/1916
War Diary	Bouzincourt	16/07/1916	26/07/1916
War Diary	Arqueves	27/07/1916	28/07/1916
War Diary	Beauval	29/07/1916	29/07/1916
War Diary	Donquer	30/07/1916	31/07/1916
Miscellaneous	From The Officer Commanding 1/1st South Midland Field Ambulance		
Heading	1/1st S.M.F.A Aug 1916		
War Diary	Donquer	01/08/1916	09/08/1916
War Diary	Beauval	10/08/1916	10/08/1916
War Diary	Varrennes	11/08/1916	13/08/1916
War Diary	Bouzincourt	14/08/1916	28/08/1916
War Diary	Bus	29/08/1916	31/08/1916
Heading	48th Div 1/1st S.M. Field Ambulance Sept 1916		
War Diary	Bus	01/09/1916	07/09/1916
War Diary	Sarton	08/09/1916	11/09/1916
War Diary	Gezaincourt	12/09/1916	18/09/1916
War Diary	St. Hilaire	19/09/1916	23/09/1916
War Diary	Ribeaucourt	24/09/1916	29/09/1916
War Diary	Candas	30/09/1916	30/09/1916
Heading	48th Div. 1/1 S.M Field Ambulance Oct 1916		
War Diary	Humbercamps	01/10/1916	01/10/1916
War Diary	St Amand	02/10/1916	20/10/1916
War Diary	Grand Rullecourt	21/10/1916	25/10/1916
War Diary	Franviller	26/10/1916	26/10/1916
War Diary	Millencourt	27/10/1916	31/10/1916
Heading	1/1st South Midland Field Ambulance From 1st November 1916 To 30 November 1916		
War Diary	Millencourt	01/11/1916	03/11/1916
War Diary	Contalmaison	04/11/1916	30/11/1916
Heading	48th Division 1/1st S.M. Field Ambulance Dec 1916		
Heading	1/1st South Midland Field Ambulance 1st Dec 1916 To 31 Dec 1916		
War Diary	Contalmaison	01/12/1916	16/12/1916
War Diary	Baizieux	17/12/1916	28/12/1916
War Diary	Becourt Chateau	29/12/1916	31/12/1916
Heading	War Diary Of 1/1st South Midland Field Ambulance 48th Division For Period January 1st To 31st 1917 Volume 22		
War Diary	Becourt	01/01/1917	27/01/1917
War Diary	Morcourt	28/01/1917	31/01/1917
Heading	48th Div 1/1st S.M Field Ambulance		
Miscellaneous	Appx 1&1a		
Heading	War Diary Of 1/1st South Midland Field Ambulance Period 1.2.17 To 28.2.17		
War Diary	Morcourt	01/02/1917	02/02/1917
War Diary	Cappy	03/02/1917	28/02/1917
Heading	48th Div. 1/1st South Midland Field Ambulance War Diary From 1st March 1917 To 31st March 1917		

War Diary	Cappy	01/03/1917	26/03/1917
War Diary	Perronne	27/03/1917	31/03/1917
Heading	48th Div. 1/1st South Midland F.A.		
Heading	1/1st South Midland Field Ambulance War Diary From 1st April 1917 To 30th April 1917		
War Diary	Perronne	01/04/1917	30/04/1917
Heading	48th Div.1/1st South Midland F.A.		
Heading	1/1st South Midland Field Ambulance War Diary From 1st May 1917 To 31 May 1917		
War Diary	Perronne	01/05/1917	13/05/1917
War Diary	Combles	14/05/1917	14/05/1917
War Diary	Beugny	15/05/1917	31/05/1917
Operation(al) Order(s)	144th Infantry Brigade Order No. 177	12/05/1917	12/05/1917
Operation(al) Order(s)	144th Infantry Bde Order No. 178	13/05/1917	13/05/1917
Miscellaneous	Relief Of 11th Division By 48th Division		
Heading	1/1st South Mid F.A.		
Heading	1/1st South Midland Field Ambulance War Diary 1st June 1917 To 30th June 1917		
War Diary	Beugny	01/06/1917	30/06/1917
Heading	War Diary 1/1st South Midland Field Ambulance From 1st July 1917 To 31st July 1917		
War Diary	Beugny	01/07/1917	02/07/1917
War Diary	Achiet Le Petit	03/07/1917	03/07/1917
War Diary	Guadiempre	04/07/1917	23/07/1917
War Diary	Guadiempre	23/07/1917	31/07/1917
Miscellaneous	Relief Of 48th Division By 3rd Division	29/06/1917	29/06/1917
Miscellaneous	Reference Maps Sheet 57D And 51c	02/07/1917	02/07/1917
Diagram etc	Diagram		
Heading	1/1st South Midland F.A.		
Heading	War Diary 1/1st South Midland Field Ambulance 1st August 1917 To 31st August 1917		
War Diary	Gwent Farm	01/08/1917	05/08/1917
War Diary	Duhallow	06/08/1917	29/08/1917
War Diary	Gwent Farm	30/08/1917	30/08/1917
War Diary	Duhallow	06/08/1917	29/08/1917
War Diary	Gwent Farm	30/08/1917	31/08/1917
Operation(al) Order(s)	R.A.M.C. 48th Division Operation Order No. 2	04/08/1917	04/08/1917
Operation(al) Order(s)	R.A.M.C. 48th Division Operation Order No. 3	11/08/1917	11/08/1917
Operation(al) Order(s)	R.A.M.C. 48th Division Operation Order No. 4	27/08/1917	27/08/1917
Miscellaneous	To Accompany 48th Division R.A.M.C. Operation Order No. 3	11/08/1917	11/08/1917
Heading	1/1st South Midland F.A.		
Heading	War Diary 1/1st South Midland Field Ambulance 1st September 1917 To 30th September 1917		
War Diary	Gwent Farm	01/09/1917	17/09/1917
War Diary	Cras Payelle	18/09/1917	30/09/1917
Operation(al) Order(s)	48th Division R.A.M.C. Operation Order No. 5	14/09/1917	14/09/1917
Miscellaneous	Addendum R.A.M.C. Operation Order No. 5	14/09/1917	14/09/1917
Miscellaneous	Transport Movement Table To Accompany 48th Div Order No. 217	14/09/1917	14/09/1917
Operation(al) Order(s)	143rd Inf. Bde. Operation Order No. 166	15/09/1917	15/09/1917
Miscellaneous	March Table For Transport Issued With O.O 166		
Miscellaneous	Addendum No.1 To 143rd Inf. Bde. Operation Order No. 166	16/09/1917	16/09/1917
Miscellaneous	Entraining And Detraining Table Issued With Add No.1 To O.O. 166		

Miscellaneous	March Table To Entraining Station (Issued With Addendum No.1 To O.O. 166		
Miscellaneous	48th Division R.A.M.C. Order By Lt-Colonel T.A. Green , R.A.M.C.T.A/A.D.M.S.	18/09/1917	18/09/1917
Miscellaneous	O.C. 1/1 S.M. Fd Ambce	24/09/1917	24/09/1917
Miscellaneous	48th Division R.A.M.C. Order By Lt-Colonel T.A. Green, R.A.M.C. TF. A/A.D.M.S. 48th Division	24/09/1917	24/09/1917
Miscellaneous	48th Division R.A.M.C. Order by Lt-Colonel T.A. Green, RAMC. T. A/A.D.M.S. 48th Division	25/09/1917	25/09/1917
Miscellaneous	C Form Messages And Signals		
Miscellaneous	Orders For Move Of Division In Connection With Addendum No.1 To 48th Division Order No. 218	26/09/1917	26/09/1917
Operation(al) Order(s)	143rd Inf. Bde Operation Order No. 107	28/09/1917	28/09/1917
Miscellaneous	Entraining Table Issued With 143rd Inf. Bde. O.O 167		
Miscellaneous	Addendum No.1 To 143rd Infantry Brigade Operation Order No. 167	29/09/1917	29/09/1917
Heading	1/1st South Midland F.A.		
Heading	War Diary 1/1st South Midland Field Amble 1st October 1917 To 31 October 1917		
War Diary	L' Abbe Farm	01/10/1917	01/10/1917
War Diary	Gwent Farm	02/10/1917	03/10/1917
War Diary	A.D.P Duhallow	03/10/1917	10/10/1917
War Diary	Sewood Camp	11/10/1917	13/10/1917
War Diary	Ligny St Flochel	14/10/1917	14/10/1917
War Diary	Villers St Simon	15/10/1917	15/10/1917
War Diary	Fresnicourt	16/10/1917	31/10/1917
Operation(al) Order(s)	48th Division R.A.M.C. Operation Order No. 7 By Colonel R. Pickard C.M.G. A.M.S A.D.M.S 48th Division	03/10/1917	03/10/1917
Operation(al) Order(s)	48th Division Operation Order No. 9 By Colonel R. Pickard C.M.G., A.M.S	07/10/1917	07/10/1917
Operation(al) Order(s)	48th Division R.A.M.C. Operation Order No. 10	09/10/1917	09/10/1917
Operation(al) Order(s)	48th Division R.A.M.C. Operation Order No. 192 By Colonel R. Pickard C.M.G., A.M.S	11/10/1917	11/10/1917
Operation(al) Order(s)	R.A.M.C. 48th Division Operation Order No. 11	14/10/1917	14/10/1917
Miscellaneous	48th Division Medical Arrangements	14/10/1917	14/10/1917

WO95/2752/1

1/1 South Midland Field Ambulance

48TH DIVISION

1-1ST STH MID'D FLD AMB.

APR 1915-~~DEC 1918~~ 1917 OCT

FROM [illegible] DIV

TO ITALY

121/5204
30th March 1915
April 1915

48

121/5204

1/1st S.M. Field Ambulance

Vol I.

Apr '15
Dec '18

Instructions regarding War Diaries and Intelligence Summaries are contained in F. S. Regs., Part II. and the Staff Manual respectively. Title pages will be prepared in manuscript.

WAR DIARY

~~or~~

~~INTELLIGENCE SUMMARY~~

(Erase heading not required.)

Army Form C. 2118.

Hour, Date, Place	Summary of Events and Information	Remarks and references to Appendices
8 a.m. 30.3.15 HARVE	Unit arrived in France & entrained for Oudezeele at 3.0 p.m.	
4 a.m. 1.4.15 CASSEL	Unit detrained & proceeded by March Route to Oudezeele.	
1.4.15 to 4.4.15. OUDEZEELE	A Small Sick Station was formed in the local School-room. Route Marches & Field Work carried out. Sanitation of Billets etc.	
5.4.15. 7 pm. BAILLEUL	Arrived here by March Route. Sick Station formed. Field Work Sanitation of Billeting Area carried out.	
1.30 p.m. 10.4.15. BAILLEUL	Proceeded by March Route to ARMENTIERES for attachment to 6th Division for course of instruction in Hospital Duties, Collecting of Wounded from Aid Posts & Advanced Dressing Stations	
11.4.15 to 16.4.15. ARMENTIERES.	Sections were detailed daily to attend at the 17th & 18th Field Ambulances for instruction	

Instructions regarding War Diaries and Intelligence Summaries are contained in F. S. Regs., Part II. and the Staff Manual respectively. Title pages will be prepared in manuscript.

WAR DIARY
or
INTELLIGENCE SUMMARY.
(Erase heading not required.)

Army Form C. 2118.

Hour, Date, Place	Summary of Events and Information	Remarks and references to Appendices
11.4.15 to 16.4.15 ARMENTIERES.	in their various duties, in connection with the organization of a Stationary Hospital. Squads were detailed from the Bearer Sub-Division of each Section to attend the various Aid Posts & Advanced Dressing Stations & work in conjunction with the South Mid. 1st & 3rd Field Ambulances. This work proved interesting & instructive.	
17.4.15. 6. pm. ROMARIN. to	Unit arrived here. Formation of Sick Collecting Station.	
30.4.15. ROMARIN	Daily Routine carried out. Sanitation of ditches, billets, etc. Bathing House formed for the washing of patients & members of this Unit. Lectures and Demonstrations on the treatment of Asphyxia. Lectures on "Sanitation". The general.	

Army Form C. 2118.

Instructions regarding War Diaries and Intelligence Summaries are contained in F. S. Regs., Part II. and the Staff Manual respectively. Title pages will be prepared in manuscript.

WAR DIARY
or
INTELLIGENCE SUMMARY.

(*Erase heading not required.*)

Hour, Date, Place	Summary of Events and Information	Remarks and references to Appendices
30.4.15 ROMARIN	principles of sanitation + the importance of same, impressed upon all ranks.	
	Cyril Hawkins LIEUT. COL. R.A.M.C.T. COMMANDING, 1st S.M.F. AMBULANCE. (Imperial Service Unit.)	

(9 29 6) W2794 100,000 8/14 H W V Forms/C. 2118/11

121/5444
May 1915

48th Div

121/5444

1st S.M. Field Ambulance

Vol II

'Instructions regarding War Diaries and Intelligence Summaries are contained in F. S. Regs., Part II. and the Staff Manual respectively. Title pages will be prepared in manuscript.

WAR DIARY
or
~~INTELLIGENCE SUMMARY~~.
(Erase heading not required.)

Army Form C. 2118.

Hour, Date, Place	Summary of Events and Information	Remarks and references to Appendices
1.5.15. ROMARIN.	Ordinary Routine Work Carried out. Sanitation of Billets etc.	
2.5.15. ROMARIN.	CHURCH Services for Unit. Tents were unpacked in order to dry + air same.	
3.5.15 ROMARIN.	Routine work Carried out. Detachment of N.C.Os and men sent to PONT DE NIEPPE to Clean Schools + and make the necessary preparations for same to be used as Hospital.	
8.30 a.m. 4.5.15 ROMARIN.	Unit moved by march route to PONT DE NIEPPE. to take over Schools for billets + Hospital.	
5.5.15 PONT DE NIEPPE	"C" Section in Charge of Hospital for sick + wounded Cases, also <u>Accomodation</u> Sick Wounded { Separate Wards 60; Officers Ward 2; Officers Ward 2 } "B" + "A" Sections general fatigues, generally cleaning up of windows, whitewashing Ceilings, sanitation of drains etc. Advanced Dressing Station LE BIZET. The necessary personnel in charge + the Ambulances brought in the sick + wounded Cases to PONT DE NIEPPE night + morning.	
6.5.15 PONT DE NIEPPE	Ordinary Routine Work. Officers Commanding Sections working independantly.	

(73989) W4141—463. 400,000. 9/14. H.&J.Ltd. Forms/C. 2118/10.

Instructions regarding War Diaries and Intelligence Summaries are contained in F. S. Regs., Part II. and the Staff Manual respectively. Title pages will be prepared in manuscript.

WAR DIARY
or
~~INTELLIGENCE SUMMARY.~~
(Erase heading not required.)

Army Form C. 2118.

Hour, Date, Place	Summary of Events and Information	Remarks and references to Appendices
7.5.15. PONT. DE NIEPPE	Routine work carried out. Inspection of harness by Commanding Officer. Lecture on the use of "Respirator".	
8.5.15 PONT DE NIEPPE	Work arranged by O.C. Sections. Tents unpacked & exposed to the air for some hours, & repacked. Unit paraded at 12.45 noon & attended the Divisional Baths at PONT DE NIEPPE.	
9.5.15. PONT. DE NIEPPE	Usual Church Services held & ordinary routine work carried out.	
10.5.15. PONT. DE NIEPPE	"B" Section relieved "C" Section in Hospital duty. Usual work arranged by O.C. Sections. Index Maps explained to N.C.O.s	
11.5.15. PONT. DE NIEPPE.	Route March during the morning. Usual Routine Work. Consultation with A.D.M.S. re Reg. aid Pts.	Appendix I
12.5.15 PONT. DE NIEPPE	Routine Work. The personnel at Advanced Dressing Station LA BIZET returned to Headquarters owing to new arrangements regarding the collection of the sick and wounded.	

(73989) W4141—463. 400,000. 9/14. H.&J.Ltd. Forms/C. 2118/10.

Instructions regarding War Diaries and Intelligence Summaries are contained in F. S. Regs., Part II. and the Staff Manual respectively. Title pages will be prepared in manuscript.

WAR DIARY
or
INTELLIGENCE SUMMARY.
(Erase heading not required.)

Army Form C. 2118.

Hour, Date, Place	Summary of Events and Information	Remarks and references to Appendices
13.5.15 PONT DE NIEPPE	Routine Work. Lectures & demonstration on the application of First Field Dressings to the Mechanical Transport A.S.C. Drivers.	
14.5.15. PONT. DE NIEPPE	Routine Work. Lieut Thomason attached to 7th Worces Regt for temporary duty, during the absence of their R.M. Officer on sick leave. Brigadier General Comdg. 144th Infantry Brigade visit the Ambulance.	
15.5.15. PONT. DE NIEPPE.	Routine Work. Unit paraded for Bathing at Divisional Baths. Lecture on "Gas Poisoning" to Officers & N.C.O.s of the 7th Worcestershire Regiment.	
16.5.15. PONT DE NIEPPE.	Routine Work. Church Parade for C of E. Free Church & R.C. Troops.	
17.5.15. PONT DE NIEPPE.	Routine Work. 2 N.C.Os & 20 men detailed to assist 1st Field Coy R.E. in making Regimental Dug Outs. Inspection of Horses & Harness of Unit by Commanding Officer. Instructions on "Respirators" by Officer Comdg. Lectures	

(73989) W4141—463. 400,000. 9/14. H.&J.Ltd. Forms/C. 2118/10.

Instructions regarding War Diaries and Intelligence Summaries are contained in F. S. Regs., Part II. and the Staff Manual respectively. Title pages will be prepared in manuscript.

WAR DIARY
or
INTELLIGENCE SUMMARY.
(*Erase heading not required.*)

Army Form C. 2118.

Hour, Date, Place	Summary of Events and Information	Remarks and references to Appendices
18.5.15. Pont de Nieppe.	Routine Work.	
19.5.15. Pont. de Nieppe.	Routine Work.	
20.5.15 Pont. de Nieppe.	Usual Routine Work performed.	
21.5.15. Pont de Nieppe	Usual Routine Work performed	
22.5.15. Pont de Nieppe	Usual Routine Work performed.	
23.5.15 Pont de Nieppe	Routine Work. Inspection by A.D.M.S 48th Division. Church Services for C of E, Free Church & R.C. members.	
24.5.15 Pont de Nieppe.	Routine Work. "C" Section detailed in charge of New Baths at Pont de Nieppe. General Sanitation of Premises carried out.	
25.5.15. Pont de Nieppe	Routine Work. Lieut Thomason returned to duty with this Unit. The Medical Officer of the 4th Norfolk Regt having returned to duty.	
26.5.15. Pont de Nieppe 27.5.15 Pont de Nieppe 28.5.15. Pont de Nieppe 29.5.15. Pont de Nieppe	Usual Routine Work carried out.	

(73989) W4141—463. 400,000. 9/14. H.&J.Ltd. Forms/C. 2118/10.

Army Form C. 2118.

Instructions regarding War Diaries and Intelligence Summaries are contained in F. S. Regs., Part II. and the Staff Manual respectively. Title pages will be prepared in manuscript.

WAR DIARY
or
INTELLIGENCE SUMMARY.

(*Erase heading not required.*)

Hour, Date, Place	Summary of Events and Information	Remarks and references to Appendices
30.5.15. PONT DE NIEPPE	Usual Routine Work performed. "Bathing" Parade at the Divisional Baths PONT DE NIEPPE. Church Services held for the various Denominations	
31.5.15 PONT DE NIEPPE	Routine Work. Lectures & Demonstrations on "Respirators" by O.C. Sections	

Cyril H. Howkins
Lt Col
OC. 1st N. Mid. F. Amb.

(73989) W4141—463. 400,000. 9/14. H.&J.Ltd. Forms/C. 2118/10.

Appendix I.

It was decided to have Regimental Aid Posts nearer the trenches – about 400–500 yds away & to evacuate from there to the present Reg Aid Post which would then become Advanced Dressing Stations.

The new Regimental A. Posts, 3 in number will be connected with the trenches by a trench. Two of these Reg. A. Posts will be dug out, then roofed in & are to measure 9 x 12 ft. superficial area, with recess for stores (med & surg.). The third Reg Aid Post will be a shell proof shelter.

These medical arrangements are connection with the Gloucester & Worcester I. Brig. (144 I. Brig).

Places where Reg. A. P. will be formed —

Ref Map 1/10000 Joined Sheets No 28 & 36. — C.3. d. 1.8. – U. 27 a. 9.8. – U 27. a. 8. 2. Situations of Adv. Dress Stat. — C. 2. d. 5. 4. – U 26 b 7.3.

C Hon[illegible]

[illegible]

June 1915

48th Division

War Diary

1st South Midland Field Ambulance.

Vol: III.

Instructions regarding War Diaries and Intelligence Summaries are contained in F. S. Regs., Part II. and the Staff Manual respectively. Title pages will be prepared in manuscript.

WAR DIARY
or
~~INTELLIGENCE SUMMARY.~~
(Erase heading not required.)

Army Form C. 2118.

Hour, Date, Place	Summary of Events and Information	Remarks and references to Appendices
1.6.15. Pont de Nieppe.	Usual Routine Work. O.C. Sections read to all N.C.O.s & men of their Sections "Memorandum on Gases".	
2.6.15. Pont de Nieppe.	Usual Routine Work. Practise in adjusting Respirators. Route March by Transport.	
3.6.15. Pont de Nieppe.	Inspection of Transport by Commanding Officer. Usual Routine Work. Inspection of Motor Ambulances.	
4.6.15. Pont de Nieppe.	Usual Routine Work performed.	
5.6.15. Pont de Nieppe.	Usual Routine Work performed.	
6.6.15. Pont de Nieppe.	Usual Routine Work performed. Church Parade for C. of E. Free Church & R.C. Troops.	
7.6.15. Pont de Nieppe.	Routine Work. Route March by Transport. "A" Section will hold themselves in readiness to proceed on Sanitary Duties.	
8.6.15. Pont de Nieppe.	Routine Work. [illegible] Parties not detailed, the [illegible] for the detention of sick wounded being completed.	
9.6.15. Pont de Nieppe.	Routine Work. Inspection of Motor Ambulances.	
10.6.15. Pont de Nieppe.	Routine Work performed.	

Instructions regarding War Diaries and Intelligence Summaries are contained in F. S. Regs., Part II. and the Staff Manual respectively. Title pages will be prepared in manuscript.

WAR DIARY
or
~~INTELLIGENCE SUMMARY.~~
(Erase heading not required.)

Army Form C. 2118.

Hour, Date, Place	Summary of Events and Information	Remarks and references to Appendices
11.6.15. Pont de Nieppe	Pontoon Work. Route March by transport. Signaller parade for practice	
12.6.15 Pont de Nieppe.	Pontoon Work. Respirator practice	
13.6.15 Pont de Nieppe.	Pontoon Work. Lieut. H P Thomason attached for temporary duty to the 1st Gloucester Regt. Divine Service for C of E. [illegible] R.C. troops	
14.6.15 Pont de Nieppe	Pontoon Work. Route March by transport.	
15.6.15 Pont de Nieppe	Pontoon Work. Inspection of [illegible] of Respirators. Respirator practice. Orders issued that only the respirator smoke helmets issued by the Ordnance Dept are to be used.	
16.6.15. Pont de Nieppe	Pontoon Work. Route March by transport.	
17.6.15 Pont de Nieppe.	Pontoon Work. Inspection of Motor [illegible].	
18.6.15. Pont de Nieppe	Pontoon Work. Route March by transport. Inspection of transport by Commanding Officer.	
19.6.15 Pont de Nieppe	Pontoon Work. Inspection of Clothing by the Quartermaster	

(73989) W4141—463. 400,000. 9/14. H.&J.Ltd. Forms/C. 2118/10.

Instructions regarding War Diaries and Intelligence Summaries are contained in F. S. Regs., Part II. and the Staff Manual respectively. Title pages will be prepared in manuscript.

WAR DIARY
or
~~INTELLIGENCE SUMMARY.~~
(Erase heading not required.)

Army Form C. 2118.

Hour, Date, Place	Summary of Events and Information	Remarks and references to Appendices
20.6.15 Pont de Nieppe	Routine Work. Church Parade for C of E, Free Church & R.C. troops	
21.6.15 Pont de Nieppe	Routine Work. Parts drawn for transport. Restoration Drill.	
22.6.15 Pont de Nieppe.	Routine Work. Inspection of First Field Dressings	
23.6.15 Pont de Nieppe.	Routine Work. Inspection of Clothing by Quartermaster. Parts drawn for transport.	
24.6.15. Pont de Nieppe.	Received orders to move off by March Route with 145th Infantry Brigade. [illegible] [illegible] Proceeded by March Route to BAILLEUL to OUTERSTEEN Rd, Cross roads METEREN – NOOTEROOME, 100 yards N.W. of cross roads.	
25.6.15	Proceeded by March Route to VIEUX BERQUIN	
26.6.15 Vieux Berquin.	Proceeded by March Route via Neuf Berquin, MERVILLE, CALONNE, ROBECQ to GONNEHEN.	
27.6.15 Gonnehen	Proceeded by March Route to ALLOUAGNE.	

(73989) W4141—463. 400,000. 9/14. H.&J.Ltd. Forms/C. 2118/10.

Instructions regarding War Diaries and Intelligence Summaries are contained in F. S. Regs., Part II. and the Staff Manual respectively. Title pages will be prepared in manuscript.

WAR DIARY

or

~~INTELLIGENCE SUMMARY.~~

(Erase heading not required.)

Army Form C. 2118.

Hour, Date, Place	Summary of Events and Information	Remarks and references to Appendices
28. 6. 15 ALLOUAGNE	Formed Hospital in School Room. General fatigues in Cleaning Billets & Sanitation &c.	
29. 6. 15 ALLOUAGNE	Routine Work. General fatigues.	
30. 6. 15 ALLOUAGNE	Routine Work. General fatigues.	

C Hawkins
Lt Col
O.C. 1st S.M. F. Amb.

121/6242

July '15

48th Division.

121/6242

1st S.M. Field Ambulance

Vol IV

Instructions regarding War Diaries and Intelligence Summaries are contained in F. S. Regs., Part II. and the Staff Manual respectively. Title pages will be prepared in manuscript.

WAR DIARY
or
INTELLIGENCE SUMMARY.
(Erase heading not required.)

Army Form C. 2118.

Hour, Date, Place	Summary of Events and Information	Remarks and references to Appendices
ALLOUAGNE 1.7.15.	General Routine Work. Inspection of Smoke Helmets.	
ALLOUAGNE 2.7.15.	Routine Work. Route March for Transport.	
ALLOUAGNE 3.7.15.	Routine Work. Practice for Signallers.	
ALLOUAGNE 4.7.15	Church Parade for R.C. C of E & Free Church troops.	
ALLOUAGNE 5.7.15.	Usual Routine Work. (The usual Routine Work consists of one Section being in charge of Hospital & another Section in charge of the Divisional Rest Station, the remaining Section furnishing pickets & general sanitation of the billeting area carried out.)	
ALLOUAGNE 6.7.15	Routine Work. Route March for Transport Section. N.C.Os were notified to make frequent inspections of their Smoke helmets to see that the mica was not broken & also to ensure the helmets being sufficiently damp enough.	

Instructions regarding War Diaries and Intelligence Summaries are contained in F. S. Regs., Part II. and the Staff Manual respectively. Title pages will be prepared in manuscript.

WAR DIARY
or
INTELLIGENCE SUMMARY.
(*Erase heading not required.*)

Army Form C. 2118.

Hour, Date, Place	Summary of Events and Information	Remarks and references to Appendices
7.7.15. ALLOUAGNE	Routine Work. Lecture on the necessity of a further single dose of Anti-Typhoid to those men who have only had one single dose. The effect of the first dose wears off in 6 months.	
8.7.15 ALLOUAGNE	Routine Work. Inspection of Motor Ambulances to ascertain whether any repairs were necessary.	
9.7.15 ALLOUAGNE	Routine Work. Inspection of Smoke Helmets. Signallers parade for practice.	
10.7.15 ALLOUAGNE	Routine Work. Inspection of the Clothing & Equipment.	
11.7.15 ALLOUAGNE.	Routine Work. Church Parades held for C of E, Free Church & R.C. members. Orders issued regarding Captured trophies, Guns, Arms etc being government property & on no account to be sent home.	

Instructions regarding War Diaries and Intelligence Summaries are contained in F. S. Regs., Part II. and the Staff Manual respectively. Title pages will be prepared in manuscript.

WAR DIARY
or
INTELLIGENCE SUMMARY.
(Erase heading not required.)

Army Form C. 2118.

Hour, Date, Place	Summary of Events and Information	Remarks and references to Appendices
12.7.15 ALLOUAGNE	Routine Work. Inspection of Smoke Helmets. Route March for Transport Section	
13.7.15 ALLOUAGNE	Routine Work, Sanitation etc.	
14.7.15 ALLOUAGNE	Routine Work. Inspection of Clothing. Route March for Transport Section.	
15.7.15 ALLOUAGNE	All patients evacuated to Casualty Clg Station. Wagons packed. Unit moved by Marching Route to AMES. Lieut. Wilks returned to duty with this Unit from the 8th Royal Warwickshire Regiment.	
16.7.15 AMES.	Hospital formed in Local School. General Sanitation of Billeting Area. Inspection of Iron Rations.	
17.7.15 AMES.	Routine Work performed. Inspection of the Clothing by the Quartermaster	

Instructions regarding War Diaries and Intelligence Summaries are contained in F. S. Regs., Part II. and the Staff Manual respectively. Title pages will be prepared in manuscript.

WAR DIARY
or
INTELLIGENCE SUMMARY.
(Erase heading not required.)

Army Form C. 2118.

Hour, Date, Place	Summary of Events and Information	Remarks and references to Appendices
18.7.15. AMES.	Routine Work. Church Parade for the various denominations.	
19.7.15. AMES.	Routine Work. 1 N.C.O + 3 men + 1 Ambulance detailed for duty at BERGUETTE STATION during the entrainment of the 143 + 145th Brigades.	
20.7.15. AMES.	Evacuation of all sick in Hospital to Casualty Clearing Station. Wagons packed + ready to move off. 2 am. "A" Section with the whole of the transport entrained at LILLERS STATION. 5 am. "B" + "C" Sections entrained at LILLERS STATION.	
21.7.15.	Unit detrained at MONDICOURT + proceeded by March Route to SARTON.	
22.7.15. SARTON.	Formation of a Divisional Rest Station in Farm in Barns + Farm-house etc. General Sanitation + Fatigues Carried out.	

(9 29 6) W2794 100,000 8/14 H W V Forms/C. 2118/11

Instructions regarding War Diaries and Intelligence Summaries are contained in F. S. Regs., Part II. and the Staff Manual respectively. Title pages will be prepared in manuscript.

WAR DIARY
or
INTELLIGENCE SUMMARY.
(Erase heading not required.)

Army Form C. 2118.

Hour, Date, Place	Summary of Events and Information	Remarks and references to Appendices
23.7.15. SARTON.	Routine Work. Sanitation of Billets etc. which were in a filthy condition, owing to refuse being left about.	
24.7.15 SARTON.	Routine Work. Inspection of Clothing by Quarter-master. Inspection of Smoke Helmets.	
25.7.15 SARTON.	Routine Work. Church Parade for C of E. Free Church + R.C. Troops.	
26.7.15. SARTON.	Routine Work. Route March for Transport Section. Sanitation of billets + billeting area.	
27.7.15 SARTON.	Routine Work. Inspection of Motor Ambulces.	
28.7.15 SARTON.	Routine Work. Inspection of Clothing by the Quartermaster. Route March for Transport Section.	
29.7.15 SARTON.	Routine Work.	

(9 29 6) W2794 100,000 8/14 H W V Forms/C. 2118/11

Instructions regarding War Diaries and Intelligence Summaries are contained in F. S. Regs., Part II. and the Staff Manual respectively. Title pages will be prepared in manuscript.

WAR DIARY
or
INTELLIGENCE SUMMARY.
(Erase heading not required.)

Army Form C. 2118.

Hour, Date, Place	Summary of Events and Information	Remarks and references to Appendices
20.5.15 SARTON.	Routine Work. Route March carried out. Breakfast cooked en route. Returned to Headquarters at mid-day. Distance of March 13 miles.	
21.5.15 SARTON.	Routine Work. Inspection of Smoke Helmets. Inspection of Clothing by the Quartermaster.	

C Houghin [?]
Lt Col.
O.C. [illegible] F. Amb.

48th Division

121
6550

August 15

1st S.M. Field Ambulance

Vol V

From 1st to 31st Aug. 1915

Instructions regarding War Diaries and Intelligence Summaries are contained in F. S. Regs., Part II. and the Staff Manual respectively. Title pages will be prepared in manuscript.

WAR DIARY

or

~~INTELLIGENCE SUMMARY.~~

(Erase heading not required.)

Army Form C. 2118.

Hour, Date, Place	Summary of Events and Information	Remarks and references to Appendices
1.8.15. SARTON.	Routine Work. Divisional Rest Station. Church Services held for C of E. Free Church and Roman Catholics	
2.8.15 SARTON.	Routine Work. Route March for Transport Section. Inspection of Smoke Helmets.	
3.8.15 SARTON.	Route March distance 14 miles. Breakfasts Cooked en route, individually. Routine Work. "C" Section detailed & proceeded to COLINCAMP for work at the Advanced Dressing Station, and Sanitary Work in the Trenches.	
4.8.15. SARTON	Routine Work in connection with Divisional Rest Station etc.	
5.8.15 SARTON	Routine Work. Inspection of Motor Ambulances Inspection of Smoke Helmets	
6.8.15 SARTON	Hospital & Divisional Rest Station Closed down.	

Army Form C. 2118.

WAR DIARY
or
~~INTELLIGENCE SUMMARY.~~
(Erase heading not required.)

Instructions regarding War Diaries and Intelligence Summaries are contained in F. S. Regs., Part II. and the Staff Manual respectively. Title pages will be prepared in manuscript.

Hour, Date, Place	Summary of Events and Information	Remarks and references to Appendices
1.8.15. SARTON.	Routine Work. Divisional Rest Station. Church Services held for C of E. Free Church and Roman Catholics.	
2.8.15 SARTON.	Routine Work. Route March for "Sanitary" Section. Inspection of Smoke Helmets.	
3.8.15 SARTON.	Route March distance 12 miles. Breakfasts Cooked en route, individually. Routine Work. "C" Section detailed & proceeded to COLINCAMP for work at the Advanced Dressing Station, and Sanitary Work in the Trenches.	
4.8.15 SARTON	Routine Work in connection with Divisional Rest Station etc.	
5.8.15 SARTON	Routine Work. Inspection of Motor Ambulances. Inspection of Smoke Helmets.	
6.8.15 SARTON	Hospital & Divisional Rest Station Closed down.	

(73989) W4141—463. 400,000. 9/14. H.&J.Ltd. Forms/C. 2118/10.

Instructions regarding War Diaries and Intelligence Summaries are contained in F. S. Regs., Part II. and the Staff Manual respectively. Title pages will be prepared in manuscript.

WAR DIARY
or
~~INTELLIGENCE SUMMARY.~~
(Erase heading not required.)

Army Form C. 2118.

Hour, Date, Place	Summary of Events and Information	Remarks and references to Appendices
6.8.15 CORTON	All patients evacuated. Unit moved by March Route to ARQUEVES.	
7.8.15 ARQUEVES	Hospital formed in disused Farm House & adjoining buildings. The Buildings were in very dirty condition, same were cleaned up & general sanitation carried out. Water scarce. Troops warned to use the greatest economy with water supplies. Water was also ~~and~~ tested & troops informed from which wells etc the water was to be taken.	
8.8.15 ARQUEVES	Routine work & general fatigues in connection with sanitation & cleaning up billets etc. Church services for the various denominations.	
9.8.15 ARQUEVES	Routine work – Transport Route March. Lieut Wells detailed until further orders to attend	

Instructions regarding War Diaries and Intelligence Summaries are contained in F. S. Regs., Part II. and the Staff Manual respectively. Title pages will be prepared in manuscript.

WAR DIARY
or
~~INTELLIGENCE SUMMARY.~~
(Erase heading not required.)

Army Form C. 2118.

Hour, Date, Place	Summary of Events and Information	Remarks and references to Appendices
6.8.15 – CARTON	All patients evacuated. Unit moved by Ordered Route to ARQUEVES.	
7.8.15 ARQUEVES	Hospital formed in disused Farm House & adjoining buildings. The Buildings were in very dirty condition, same were cleaned up & general sanitation carried out. Water Scarce. Troops warned to use the greatest economy with Water supplies. Water was also ~~and~~ tested & troops informed from which wells etc the water was to be taken.	
8.8.15 ARQUEVES	Routine work. General fatigues in connection with sanitation & cleaning up Billets etc. Church services for the various denominations.	
9.8.15 ARQUEVES	Routine work – [illegible] Route March. Lieut Watts detailed until further orders to attend	

(73989) W4141—463. 400,000. 9/14. H.&J.Ltd. Forms/C. 2118/10.

Instructions regarding War Diaries and Intelligence Summaries are contained in F. S. Regs., Part II. and the Staff Manual respectively. Title pages will be prepared in manuscript.

WAR DIARY
or
~~INTELLIGENCE SUMMARY.~~
(Erase heading not required.)

Army Form C. 2118.

Hour, Date, Place	Summary of Events and Information	Remarks and references to Appendices
9.8.15 ARQUEVES	the rest of the 48th Div Supply Column and 48th Mobile Veterinary Section	
10.8.15 ARQUEVES	General Routine Work.	
11.8.15 ARQUEVES	General Routine Work. Smoke Helmets inspected by the Section Officer. Motor Ambulances inspected	
12.8.15 ARQUEVES	General Routine Work. Men & Wagons detailed to assist the farmers with their harvest.	
13.8.15 ARQUEVES	Routine Work - Harvesting. Inspection of Rifles of the M.T.A.S.C.	
14.8.15 ARQUEVES	Routine Work - Harvesting. Inspection of Clothing.	
15.8.15 ARQUEVES	Routine Work - Harvesting. Church Services for C of E & R.C. troops.	
16.8.15 ARQUEVES	Routine Work - Harvesting. Inspection of Smoke Helmets	

(9 29 6) W2794 100,000 8/14 H W V Forms/C. 2118/11

Instructions regarding War Diaries and Intelligence Summaries are contained in F. S. Regs., Part II. and the Staff Manual respectively. Title pages will be prepared in manuscript.

WAR DIARY
or
~~INTELLIGENCE SUMMARY.~~
(Erase heading not required.)

Army Form C. 2118.

Hour, Date, Place	Summary of Events and Information	Remarks and references to Appendices
9.8.15 ARQUEVES	the rest of the 48th Div. Supply Column and 48th Mobile Veterinary Section	
10.8.15 ARQUEVES.	General Routine Work.	
11.8.15 ARQUEVES	General Routine Work. Smoke Helmets inspected by the Section Officer. Motor Ambulances inspected	
12.8.15 ARQUEVES.	General Routine Work. Men & Wagons detailed to assist the farmers with their harvest	
13.8.15 ARQUEVES.	Routine Work – Harvesting. Inspection of Rifles of the M.T.A.S.C.	
14.8.15 ARQUEVES.	Routine Work – Harvesting. Inspection of Clothing.	
15.8.15 ARQUEVES	Routine Work – Harvesting. Church Service for C of E & R.C. troops.	
16.8.15 ARQUEVES	Routine Work – Harvesting. Inspection of Smoke Helmets.	

Army Form C. 2118.

Instructions regarding War Diaries and Intelligence Summaries are contained in F. S. Regs., Part II. and the Staff Manual respectively. Title pages will be prepared in manuscript.

WAR DIARY
or
INTELLIGENCE SUMMARY.
(Erase heading not required.)

Hour, Date, Place	Summary of Events and Information	Remarks and references to Appendices
17.8.15 ARQUEVES.	Routine Work. Harvesting. Rifle inspection M.T.A.S.C. Signallers practice.	
18.8.15 ARQUEVES.	Routine Work. Harvesting. Route March for transport. Inspection of Clothing.	
19.8.15 ARQUEVES.	Routine Work. Harvesting. Inspection of Motor Ambce. Inspection of Smoke-Helmets.	
20.8.15 ARQUEVES.	Routine Work. Harvesting. Inspection of Transport by Commanding Officer.	
21.8.15 ARQUEVES.	Routine Work. Harvesting. Inspection of Clothing.	
22.8.15 ARQUEVES.	Routine Work. Church Services for R.C. & C of E troops. Harvesting.	
23.8.15 ARQUEVES.	Routine Work. Inspection of Smoke-Helmets. Harvesting.	
24.8.15 ARQUEVES.	Routine Work. Inspection of Rifles of M.T.A.S.C. Signallers parade for practice.	

(9 29 6) W 2794 100,000 8/14 H W V Forms/C. 2118/11

WAR DIARY
or
INTELLIGENCE ~~SUMMARY.~~
(Erase heading not required.)

Army Form C. 2118.

Instructions regarding War Diaries and Intelligence Summaries are contained in F. S. Regs., Part II. and the Staff Manual respectively. Title pages will be prepared in manuscript.

Hour, Date, Place	Summary of Events and Information	Remarks and references to Appendices
17.8.15 ARQUEVES.	Routine Work. – Harvesting. Rifle Inspection M.T.A.S.C. Signallers practice.	
18.8.15 ARQUEVES.	Routine Work – Harvesting. Route March for Transport. Inspection of Clothing	
19.8.15 ARQUEVES.	Routine Work. Harvesting. Inspection of Motor Ambulance. Inspection of Smoke-Helmets.	
20.8.15 ARQUEVES.	Routine Work. – Harvesting. – Inspection of Transport by Commanding Officer	
21.8.15 ARQUEVES.	Routine Work. – Harvesting – Inspection of Clothing.	
22.8.15 ARQUEVES.	Routine Work. Church Service for R.C. & C of E troops – Harvesting	
23.8.15 ARQUEVES	Routine Work. – Inspection of Smoke-Helmets – Harvesting.	
24.8.15 ARQUEVES.	Routine Work. Inspection of Rifles of M.T.A.S.C. Signallers parade for practice.	

(73989) W4141—463. 400,000. 9/14. H.&J.Ltd. Forms/C. 2118/10.

Instructions regarding War Diaries and Intelligence Summaries are contained in F. S. Regs., Part II. and the Staff Manual respectively. Title pages will be prepared in manuscript.

WAR DIARY

or

~~INTELLIGENCE SUMMARY.~~

(Erase heading not required.)

Army Form C. 2118.

Hour, Date, Place	Summary of Events and Information	Remarks and references to Appendices
25. 8. 15 ARQUEVES.	Routine Work. Inspection of Clothing Harvesting.	
26. 8. 15 ARQUEVES.	Routine Work. Harvesting. The Adv. Dress. Station Attachment returned, as part of trenches were taken over by 4th Div.	
27/8/15 ARQUEVES.	Routine Work, Harvesting.	
28/8/15 ARQUEVES	Inspection of Clothing. Harvesting. Arrival of 3 Reinforcements. Inspection by DMS., DDMS. & ADMS.	
29/8/15 ARQUEVES	Church services for various denomination Routine Work.	
30/8/15 ARQUEVES.	Routine Work. B. Section to work Hospital as arranged in RAMC Standing Orders & Not attend Corps parades.	
31/8/15 ARQUEVES.	Routine Work Harvesting.	

C Hawkins

COMMANDING [illegible] R.A.M.C. (Imperial Service Unit)

(9 29 6) W 2794 100,000 8/14 H W V Forms/C. 2118/11

Instructions regarding War Diaries and Intelligence Summaries are contained in F. S. Regs., Part II. and the Staff Manual respectively. Title pages will be prepared in manuscript.

WAR DIARY
or
~~INTELLIGENCE SUMMARY.~~
(Erase heading not required.)

Army Form C. 2118.

Hour, Date, Place	Summary of Events and Information	Remarks and references to Appendices
25. 8. 15 ARQUEVES.	Routine Work. Inspection of Clothing Harvesting.	
26 8. 15 ARQUEVES.	Routine Work. Harvesting. The Adv Dress Station Attachment returned, as part of trenches were taken over by 4th Div.	
27/8/15 ARQUEVES.	Routine work, Harvesting.	
28/8/15 ARQUEVES	Inspection of Clothing. Harvesting. Arrival of 3 Reinforcements. Inspection by DMS, DDMS & ADMS	
29/8/15 ARQUEVES	Church services for various denomination Routine work.	
30/8/15 ARQUEVES.	Routine Work. B. Section to work Hospital as arranged in RAMC Standing Orders & Not attend Corps parades.	
31/8/15 ARQUEVES.	Routine Work Harvesting.	

C Hawkins
.... LIEUT. COL. R.A.M.C.T.
COMMANDING, 1st S.M.F. AMBULANCE.
(Imperial Service Unit.)

(73989) W4141—463. 400,000. 9/14. H.&J.Ltd. Forms/C. 2118/10.

11 48th Division

121
6971

Sept 115

1/1st S.M. Field Ambulance

Vol VI

Sept. 15

Instructions regarding War Diaries and Intelligence Summaries are contained in F. S. Regs., Part II. and the Staff Manual respectively. Title pages will be prepared in manuscript.

WAR DIARY
or
~~INTELLIGENCE SUMMARY~~.
(Erase heading not required.)

Army Form C. 2118.

Hour, Date, Place	Summary of Events and Information	Remarks and references to Appendices
1.9.15. ARQUEVES.	General Routine Work. Inspection of Clothing	
2.9.15 ARQUEVES.	General Routine Work. Sanitation etc. Inspection of Motor Ambulances by A.S.C. Officer.	
3.9.15 ARQUEVES.	Routine Work. Inspection of Transport by Comdg. Officer. Two Officers & a party of N.C.O's & men proceeded to the Advanced Dressing Station at FONQUEVILLERS.	
4.9.15 ARQUEVES.	General Routine Work. Inspection of Clothing by the Quartermaster	
5.9.15 ARQUEVES.	Routine Work. Divine Service for R.Co & C. of E.	
6.9.15 ARQUEVES.	Routine Work. Inspection of Smoke Helmets	
7.9.15 ARQUEVES.	Routine Work. A.S.C. M.T. drivers were inspected.	

(9 29 6) W2794 100,000 8/14 H W V Forms/C. 2118/11

Instructions regarding War Diaries and Intelligence Summaries are contained in F. S. Regs., Part II. and the Staff Manual respectively. Title pages will be prepared in manuscript.

WAR DIARY
or
~~INTELLIGENCE SUMMARY.~~
(Erase heading not required.)

Army Form C. 2118.

Hour, Date, Place	Summary of Events and Information	Remarks and references to Appendices
8.9.15 ARQUEVES.	Routine Work carried out. Inspection of Clothing by Quartermaster	
9.9.15 ARQUEVES.	Routine Work. Instruction of Motor Ambulances. Inspection of Smoke Helmets. Bath House formed in empty Farm Buildings. twenty men can bathe at one time	
10.9.15 ARQUEVES.	Routine Work. Inspection of rifles of M.T. A.S.C. drivers. Signallers [illegible] in practice	
11.9.15 ARQUEVES.	Routine Work. Inspection of Clothing by the Quartermaster. "A" Section relieved "B" Section in Hospital.	
12.9.15 ARQUEVES.	Routine Work. Divine Service. Inspection of Iron Rations	
12.9.15 ARQUEVES.	Routine Work. Inspection of Smoke Helmets. Instruction in Map Reading to N.C.O.s.	

Instructions regarding War Diaries and Intelligence Summaries are contained in F. S. Regs., Part II. and the Staff Manual respectively. Title pages will be prepared in manuscript.

WAR DIARY
or
~~INTELLIGENCE SUMMARY.~~
(*Erase heading not required.*)

Army Form C. 2118.

Hour, Date, Place	Summary of Events and Information	Remarks and references to Appendices
14.9.15 ARQUEVES	Routine Work. Inspection of rifles of M.T.A.S.C. drivers rifles.	
15.9.15 ARQUEVES	Routine Work. Inspection of clothing by Quartermaster. Camp Canteen formed at the hospital open at 6 a.m. & again at 5 pm till 8.45 pm.	
16.9.15 ARQUEVES	Routine Work. Inspection of Motor Ambulances. Inspection of Smoke Helmets.	
17.9.15 ARQUEVES	Routine Work. Inspection of M.A.C. drivers rifles. Route March for transport.	
18.9.15 ARQUEVES	Routine Work. Inspection of clothing by Quartermaster.	
19.9.15 ARQUEVES	Routine Work. Divine Service.	
20.9.15 ARQUEVES	Routine Work. Inspection of Smoke Helmets.	
2.9.15 ARQUEVES	Routine Work. Inspection of M.A.C. drivers rifles.	

Army Form C. 2118.

Instructions regarding War Diaries and Intelligence Summaries are contained in F. S. Regs., Part II. and the Staff Manual respectively. Title pages will be prepared in manuscript.

WAR DIARY
or
INTELLIGENCE SUMMARY.
(Erase heading not required.)

Hour, Date, Place	Summary of Events and Information	Remarks and references to Appendices
21.9.15 ARQUEVES.	1 Officer, 1 N.C.O + 12 men proceeded to COUIN to take charge of the Baths	
22.9.15 ARQUEVES.	Routine Work. Inspection of Clothing by Quartermaster	
23.9.15 ARQUEVES.	Routine Work. Inspection of Smoke-Helmets. Inspection of [illegible]. Medical Store Carts Wagons packed as far as possible in case of a forward move.	
24.9.15 ARQUEVES.	Routine Work. Inspection of [illegible] [illegible]	
25.9.15 ARQUEVES.	Routine Work. Inspection of Clothing by Quarter-master	
26.9.15 ARQUEVES.	Routine Work. Divine Service. All Smoke Helmets inspected in case of a forward move which was expected	

(9 29 6) W2794 100,000 8/14 H W V Forms/C. 2118/11

Instructions regarding War Diaries and Intelligence Summaries are contained in F. S. Regs., Part II. and the Staff Manual respectively. Title pages will be prepared in manuscript.

WAR DIARY
or
~~INTELLIGENCE SUMMARY.~~
(Erase heading not required.)

Army Form C. 2118.

Hour, Date, Place	Summary of Events and Information	Remarks and references to Appendices
27.9.15. ARQUEVES.	Routine Work. All barns etc which could be utilised for the reception of sick, in case of heavy fighting, were cleaned up & fresh straw etc laid down. Accommodation was made for approximately 1000 cases.	
28.9.15 ARQUEVES	Routine Work – Inspection of Smoke Helmets	
29.9.15 ARQUEVES	Routine Work. Inspection of Clothing by Quartermaster	
30.9.15 ARQUEVES.	Routine Work. Inspection of Motor Ambulances. Inspection of Smoke Helmets.	

C. Hawkins
LIEUT. COL. R.A.M.C.T.
COMMANDING, 1st S.M.F. AMBULANCE
(Imperial Service Unit.)

Oct 1915

48th Division

121
7449

1/1 SM
(S.M.) Fd. Amb.

Oct. - 15

Vol VII

Instructions regarding War Diaries and Intelligence Summaries are contained in F. S. Regs., Part II. and the Staff Manual respectively. Title pages will be prepared in manuscript.

WAR DIARY

or

~~INTELLIGENCE SUMMARY.~~

(Erase heading not required.)

Army Form C. 2118.

Hour, Date, Place	Summary of Events and Information	Remarks and references to Appendices
1.10.15. ARQUEVES.	Routine Work. Inspection of M.T. A.S.C. drivers rifles. Route March for Transport	
2.10.15 ARQUEVES.	Routine Work. Route March for all available men	
3.10.15 ARQUEVES.	Routine Work. Church Service.	
4.10.15 ARQUEVES.	Routine Work. Work arranged by O.C. Sections. Inspection of Smoke Helmets Transport route march.	
5.10.15 ARQUEVES.	Routine Work. Work arranged by O.C. Sections	
6.10.15. ARQUEVES.	Routine Work. Route March for Transport. Inspection of Clothing by Quartermaster	
7.10.15 ARQUEVES.	Routine Work. Inspection of Smoke Helmets. Inspection of Motor Ambulances.	
8.10.15 ARQUEVES.	Routine Work. Inspection of Transport by Commanding Officer. Inspection of	

(9 29 6) W 2794 100,000 8/14 H W V Forms/C. 2118/11

Instructions regarding War Diaries and Intelligence Summaries are contained in F. S. Regs., Part II. and the Staff Manual respectively. Title pages will be prepared in manuscript.

WAR DIARY
or
INTELLIGENCE SUMMARY.
(Erase heading not required.)

Army Form C. 2118.

Hour, Date, Place	Summary of Events and Information	Remarks and references to Appendices
8.10.15 ARQUEVES.	Drill. N.C.Os. draws rifles.	
9.10.15 ARQUEVES.	Routine Work. Inspection of Clothing by Quartermaster. Work arranged by O.C. Sections	
10.10.15 ARQUEVES.	Routine Work. Church Service. Instruction given to N.C.Os & men regarding the safe custody of their regimental badges & shoulder titles	
11.10.15 ARQUEVES.	Routine Work. Work arranged by O.C. Sections. Inspection of Smoke Helmets	
12.10.15 ARQUEVES.	Routine Work, arranged by O.C. Sections. Inspection of rifles of the Motor Ambulances.	
13.10.15 ARQUEVES.	Routine Work arranged by O.C. Sections. Inspection of Clothing by Quartermaster	
14.10.15 ARQUEVES.	Routine Work arranged by O.C. Sections. Demonstration on "How to adjust the	

(9 29 6) W2794 100,000 8/14 H W V Forms/C. 2118/11

Instructions regarding War Diaries and Intelligence Summaries are contained in F. S. Regs., Part II. and the Staff Manual respectively. Title pages will be prepared in manuscript.

WAR DIARY
or
~~INTELLIGENCE SUMMARY.~~
(Erase heading not required.)

Army Form C. 2118.

Hour, Date, Place	Summary of Events and Information	Remarks and references to Appendices
14.10.15 ARQUEVES.	new Tube Helmets. Inspection of Motor Ambulance by the O.C. Field Amb. Workshop Unit. Inspection of Smoke Helmets.	
15.10.15 ARQUEVES.	Routine Work in O.C. Sections. "B" Section relieved "A" Section at the Advanced Dressing Station at FONQUEVILLERS.	
16.10.15 ARQUEVES.	Routine Work. Inspection of Clothing by Quartermaster.	
17.10.15 ARQUEVES.	Routine Work. Church Services held.	
18.10.15 ARQUEVES.	Routine Work. Inspection of Smoke Helmets.	
19.10.15 ARQUEVES.	Routine Work. Inspection of M. R. C. Drivers Rifles. Special attention called to the Saluting of Officers of the Allied Armies.	
20.10.15 ARQUEVES.	Routine Work. Inspection of Clothing	

(9 29 6) W 2794 100,000 8/14 H W V Forms/C. 2118/11

Instructions regarding War Diaries and Intelligence Summaries are contained in F. S. Regs., Part II. and the Staff Manual respectively. Title pages will be prepared in manuscript.

WAR DIARY
or
INTELLIGENCE SUMMARY.
(*Erase heading not required.*)

Army Form C. 2118.

Hour, Date, Place	Summary of Events and Information	Remarks and references to Appendices
20.11.15 ARQUEVES	by the Quartermaster.	
21.11.15 ARQUEVES	Routine Work. Inspection of Rifles & L.G. Armourer [illegible]. Inspection of Smoke Helmets.	
22.11.15 ARQUEVES	Routine Work. Inspection of Company by Commanding Officer.	
23.11.15 ARQUEVES	Routine Work. Inspection of Clothing by the Quartermaster.	
24.11.15 ARQUEVES	Routine Work. Church Service held. Issue of Winter Clothing.	
25.11.15 ARQUEVES	Routine Work. Inspection of Smoke & Tube Helmets. Fire Brigade formed. The local engine being used for drill at 2 p.m.	
26.11.15 ARQUEVES	Routine Work. Instructions issued to all men in case of a fire alarm.	

(9 29 6) W2794 100,000 8/14 H W V Forms/C. 2118/11

Army Form C. 2118.

Instructions regarding War Diaries and Intelligence Summaries are contained in F. S. Regs., Part II. and the Staff Manual respectively. Title pages will be prepared in manuscript.

WAR DIARY
or
~~INTELLIGENCE SUMMARY.~~
(Erase heading not required.)

Hour, Date, Place	Summary of Events and Information	Remarks and references to Appendices
27.10.15 ARQUEVES	Routine Work. Inspection of Clothing by Quartermaster. Capt Welts of this Unit transferred to 6th Glouces. Regt. Lieut Allison from 6th Glouces Regt to this Unit.	
28.10.15 ARQUEVES.	Routine Work. Inspection of Motor Ambces by O.C. 4? Ambce Workshop Unit. Inspection of Smoke Helmets.	
29.10.15 ARQUEVES.	Routine Work. Inspection of Men? A.S.C. driver rifles. Inspection of Transport by Commanding Officer.	
30.10.15 ARQUEVES	Routine Work. Inspection of Clothing by Quartermaster	
31.10.15 ARQUEVES	Routine Work. Church Service held.	

C. Harkins?
LIEUT. COL. R.A.M.C.
COMMANDING, 1st S.M.F. AMBULANCE.
(Imperial Service Unit.)

(9 29 6) W2794 100,000 8/14 H W V Forms/C. 2118/11

Instructions regarding War Diaries and Intelligence Summaries are contained in F. S. Regs., Part II. and the Staff Manual respectively. Title pages will be prepared in manuscript.

WAR DIARY

~~or~~

~~INTELLIGENCE SUMMARY.~~

(*Erase heading not required.*)

Army Form C. 2118.

1/1 [illegible] F Amb

Hour, Date, Place	Summary of Events and Information	Remarks and references to Appendices
1.12.15. ARQUEVES.	Routine Work. Inspection of Clothing by Quartermaster	
2.12.15 ARQUEVES.	Routine Work. Inspection of Smoke-Helmets. Inspection of Motor Ambulances by O.C. Fd Ambce Workshop Unit.	
3.12.15 ARQUEVES.	Routine Work. Inspection of M.T. A.S.C. drivers rifles. Inspection of Horse-transport by Commanding Officer.	
4.12.15. ARQUEVES.	Routine Work performed.	
5.12.15. ARQUEVES.	Routine Work. Divine Service for the various denominations.	
6.12.15 ARQUEVES.	Routine Work. Inspection of Smoke Helmets.	
7.12.15. ARQUEVES.	Routine Work. Inspection of M.T. A.S.C. drivers rifles.	
8.12.15 ARQUEVES.	Routine Work. Inspection of Clothing	

Army Form C. 2118.

Instructions regarding War Diaries and Intelligence Summaries are contained in F. S. Regs., Part II. and the Staff Manual respectively. Title pages will be prepared in manuscript.

WAR DIARY
or
INTELLIGENCE SUMMARY.
(Erase heading not required.)

Hour, Date, Place	Summary of Events and Information	Remarks and references to Appendices
9.12.15. ARQUEVES.	Routine Work. Inspection of Smoke Helmets. O.C. Fd Amble Workshop inspection of Motor Ambulances.	
10.12.15 ARQUEVES.	Routine Work. Inspection of Horse Transport by Commanding Officer. Inspection of Dn.l. A.S.C. drivers rifles	
11.12.15 ARQUEVES	Routine Work.	
12.12.15 ARQUEVES.	Routine Work. Divine Service held for various denominations. "C" Section relieved "B" Section at Advanced Dressing Station FONQUEVILLERS.	
13.12.15 ARQUEVES	Routine Work. Inspection of Smoke Helmets	
14.12.15 ARQUEVES	Routine Work. Inspection of Dn.l. A.S.C. drivers rifles	
15.12.15 ARQUEVES	Routine Work. Inspection of Clothing	

(9 29 6) W2794 100,000 8/14 H W V Forms/C. 2118/11

Instructions regarding War Diaries and Intelligence Summaries are contained in F. S. Regs., Part II. and the Staff Manual respectively. Title pages will be prepared in manuscript.

WAR DIARY
or
INTELLIGENCE SUMMARY.
(Erase heading not required.)

Army Form C. 2118.

Hour, Date, Place	Summary of Events and Information	Remarks and references to Appendices
16.12.15 ARQUEVES.	Routine Work. Inspection of Smoke Helmets. O.C. Fd Ambce Workshop Unit inspected Motor Ambulances.	
17.12.15 ARQUEVES.	Routine Work. Inspection of M.T. A.S.C. drivers rifles. Inspection of Horse Transport by Commanding Officer.	
18.12.15 ARQUEVES.	Routine Work. O.C. Sections will inspect Smoke Helmets of Service Dress Jackets & ascertain if any of them are made of thin material, if so they will be returned to Q.Mr. Stores	
19.12.15 ARQUEVES.	Routine Work. Divine Service held for various denominations	
20.12.15 ARQUEVES.	Routine Work. Inspection of Smoke Helmets.	
21.12.15 ARQUEVES.	Routine Work. Inspection of M.T. A.S.C. drivers rifles.	

(9 29 6) W2794 100,000 8/14 H W V Forms/C. 2118/11

Instructions regarding War Diaries and Intelligence Summaries are contained in F. S. Regs., Part II. and the Staff Manual respectively. Title pages will be prepared in manuscript.

WAR DIARY
or
INTELLIGENCE SUMMARY.
(Erase heading not required.)

Army Form C. 2118.

Hour, Date, Place	Summary of Events and Information	Remarks and references to Appendices
22.12.15. ARQUEVES	Routine Work. Inspection of Clothing by Quartermaster.	
23.12.15 ARQUEVES.	Routine Work. Inspection of Smoke Helmets. Inspection of Motor Ambulances by O.C. 2nd Mobile Workshop Unit.	
24.12.15 ARQUEVES.	Routine Work. Inspection of Horse Transport by Commanding Officer. Inspection of Dr. A.S.C. Drivers rifles.	
25.12.15 ARQUEVES.	Routine Work. Holy Communion. Divine Service held for various denominations. A Xmas dinner was given to the men at a suitable Café in this village.	
26.12.15. ARQUEVES.	Usual Routine work performed.	

Instructions regarding War Diaries and Intelligence Summaries are contained in F. S. Regs., Part II. and the Staff Manual respectively. Title pages will be prepared in manuscript.

WAR DIARY
or
INTELLIGENCE SUMMARY.
(Erase heading not required.)

Army Form C. 2118.

Hour, Date, Place	Summary of Events and Information	Remarks and references to Appendices
27.12.15. ARQUEVES.	Routine Work. Inspection of Smoke Helmets.	
28.12.15. ARQUEVES.	Routine Work. Inspection of M.T. A.S.C. drivers rifles.	
29.12.15 ARQUEVES.	Routine Work. Inspection of Clothing by Quartermaster.	
30.12.15. ARQUEVES.	Routine Work. Inspection of Smoke Helmets. Inspection of Motor Ambces by O.C. 2nd Ambce Workshop Unit.	
31.12.15 ARQUEVES.	Routine Work. Inspection of M.T. A.S.C. drivers rifles. Inspection of Horse Transport by Commanding Officer.	

C Hawken
LIEUT. COL. R.A.M.C.T.
COMMANDING, 1st S.M.F. AMBULANCE.
(Imperial Service Unit.)

48

1st S.M. 7th Amb.

~~Dec~~

Jan 16 Vol. IX

48

F/212/1

~~Dec 1915.~~
Jan 1916

48

1/1 SM Fd Amb

Vol X &

XIII

Jan. 1916

Instructions regarding War Diaries and Intelligence Summaries are contained in F. S. Regs., Part II. and the Staff Manual respectively. Title pages will be prepared in manuscript.

WAR DIARY

or

~~INTELLIGENCE SUMMARY~~.

(Erase heading not required.)

Army Form C. 2118.

Hour, Date, Place		Summary of Events and Information	Remarks and references to Appendices
1st Jan. 1916	ARQUÉVES	Usual Routine Work performed. Tube Helmet Instruction and Practice.	
2nd Jan 1916.	— do —	Usual Routine Work. Divine Service Held.	
3rd Jan 1916	— do —	Usual Routine Work. Inspection of Smoke Helmets and Goggles.	
4th Jan. 1916	— do —	Routine Work. Inspection of M.T. A.S.C. Drivers Rifles	
5th Jan. 1916.	— do —	Routine Work. Inspection of Clothing.	
6th Jan. 1916	— do —	Routine Work. Inspection of Motor Ambces. by Officer Commanding Fld. Ambce. Workshop Unit.	
7th Jan 1916	— do —	Routine Work. Inspection of M.T.A.S.C. Drivers Rifles.	
8th Jan 1916	— do —	Routine Work.	
9th Jan 1916	— do —	Routine Work. Divine Service held.	
10th Jan. 1916	— do —	Routine Work. Inspection of Tube Helmets	
11th Jan. 1916	— do —	Routine Work. Inspection of M.T. A.S.C. Drivers Rifles. Practice in wearing and adjusting Tube Helmets.	
12th Jan 1916	— do —	Routine Work. Inspection of Clothing by Quartermaster	
13th Jan 1916	— do —	Routine Work. Inspection of Motor Ambulances by O.C. Fld. Ambce. Workshop Unit. Inspection and demonstration of Tube Helmets.	

(73989) W4141—463. 400,000. 9/14. H.&J.Ltd. Forms/C. 2118/10.

Instructions regarding War Diaries and Intelligence Summaries are contained in F. S. Regs., Part II. and the Staff Manual respectively. Title pages will be prepared in manuscript.

WAR DIARY
or
INTELLIGENCE SUMMARY.
(Erase heading not required.)

Army Form C. 2118.

Hour, Date, Place	Summary of Events and Information	Remarks and references to Appendices
14th Jan. 1916. ARQUÉVES	Routine Work. Inspection of Horse Transport by Commanding Officers. Inspection of M.T.A.S.C. Drivers Rifles	
15th Jan. 1916. — do —	Routine Work.	
16th Jan. 1916 — do —	Routine Work. Divine Service held.	
17th Jan 1916 — do —	Routine Work. Inspection of Tube Helmets.	
18th Jan 1916 — do —	Routine Work. Inspection of M.T.A.S.C. Drivers Rifles.	
19th Jan 1916 — do —	Routine Work. Inspection of Clothing by Quartermaster	
20th Jan 1916 — do —	Routine Work. Inspection of Smoke Helmets. Inspection of Motor Ambulances by O.C. Field Amb. Workshop Unit.	
21st Jan 1916 — do —	Routine Work. Inspection of M.T.A.S.C. Drivers Rifles. CAPT. H.E. McCREADY transferred permanently as Regimental Medical Officer to 1/5th Royal Warwickshire Regt. Lieut. C DAVIES-JONES having reported for duty is taken on the strength of the Unit.	
22nd Jan 1916. — do —	Routine Work.	
23rd Jan 1916 — do —	Routine Work. Divine Service held.	
24th Jan 1916 — do —	Routine Work. Inspection and Practice adjusting Tube Helmets	
25th Jan 1916 — do —	Routine Work. Inspection of M.T.A.S.C Drivers Rifles	
26th Jan 1916 — do —	Routine Work. Inspection of Clothing	
27th Jan 1916 — do —	Routine Work. Inspection of Motor Ambces. by O.C. Field Ambulance Workshop Unit.	
28th Jan 1916 — do —	Routine Work. Inspection of Tube Helmets Inspection of M.T.A.S.C. Drivers Rifles	
29th Jan 1916 — do —	Routine Work.	

(73989) W4141—463. 400,000. 9/14. H.&J.Ltd. Forms/C. 2118/10.

Instructions regarding War Diaries and Intelligence Summaries are contained in F. S. Regs., Part II. and the Staff Manual respectively. Title pages will be prepared in manuscript.

WAR DIARY
or
INTELLIGENCE SUMMARY.
(Erase heading not required.)

Army Form C. 2118.

Hour, Date, Place	Summary of Events and Information	Remarks and references to Appendices
30th Jan 1916 ARQUÉVES.	Routine Work. Divine Service held.	
31st Jan 1916 — do —	Routine Work. Inspection and demonstration of Tube Helmets. A Dental Department was opened in the hospital the necessary equipment being provided by a private source.	

[signature]

........LIEUT. COL. R.A.M.C.T.
COMMANDING, 1st S.M.F. AMBULANCE.
(Imperial Service Unit.)

(73989) W4141—463. 400,000. 9/14. H.&J.Ltd. Forms/C. 2118/10.

48th Division

1/1 S.M. Field Ambulance

Feb 1916

48

1/1 S M Fd Amb

Feb

Vol XI

Instructions regarding War Diaries and Intelligence Summaries are contained in F. S. Regs., Part II and the Staff Manual respectively. Title pages will be prepared in manuscript.

WAR DIARY
or
~~INTELLIGENCE SUMMARY~~.
(Erase heading not required.)

Army Form C. 2118.

Hour, Date, Place	Summary of Events and Information	Remarks and references to Appendices
1.2.16 ARQUEVES.	Usual Routine Work carried out. Instruction of Motor Ambulance drivers rifles	
2.2.16 ARQUEVES.	Routine Work. Inspection of Clothing by the Quartermaster	
3.2.16 ARQUEVES.	Routine Work. Inspection of Smoke Helmets. Inspection of Motor Ambulances by O.C. Field Ambulance Workshop Unit. An Advance Party ~~under~~ a medical officer took over from the 11th Field Ambulance the Advanced Post at COLINCAMPS.	
4.2.16. ARQUEVES.	A Section proceeded to BERTRANCOURT to take over hospital formerly in charge of 11th Field Ambulance. Remainder of details left at ARQUEVES to clean up billets etc and afterwards proceeded to BERTRANCOURT.	
5.2.16. BERTRANCOURT.	Routine & fatigue work in connection with preparing the Hospital. The premises used as Hospital were formerly an Estaminet; they were quite suitable for the purpose of a Field Ambulance Hospital but rather small, additional accomodation being arranged for by the construction of Canvas Shelters.	
6.2.16 BERTRANCOURT.	Usual Routine Work. Inspection of Smoke Helmets.	
7.2.16. BERTRANCOURT.	Routine work performed.	

(73989) W4141—463. 400,000. 9/14. H.&J.Ltd. Forms/C. 2118/10.

Instructions regarding War Diaries and Intelligence Summaries are contained in F. S. Regs., Part II. and the Staff Manual respectively. Title pages will be prepared in manuscript.

WAR DIARY
or
~~INTELLIGENCE~~ SUMMARY.
(*Erase heading not required.*)

Army Form C. 2118.

Hour, Date, Place	Summary of Events and Information	Remarks and references to Appendices
8. 2. 16 BERTRANCOURT.	Usual Routine Work performed. Inspection of Motor Ambulance Drivers rifles.	
9. 2. 16 BERTRANCOURT.	Routine Work carried out.	
10. 2. 16 BERTRANCOURT.	Routine Work. Inspection of Motor Ambulances by O.C. Field Ambulance Workshops Unit.	
11. 2. 16. BERTRANCOURT.	Routine Work. The advanced dressing stations at FONQUEVILLERS + LA HAIE FARM were handed over to the 3rd S. Midland Field Ambulance, and the Advanced Dressing Station at SAILLY + HEBUTERNE were taken over by us from the 3rd S. M. Field Amblce.	
12. 2. 16. BERTRANCOURT.	Usual Routine work in connection with Hospital etc.	
13. 2. 16. BERTRANCOURT.	Routine Work. Divine Service held. Captain C. J. Broome struck off the strength having been evacuated to England on 29. 0. 15 (Authority D.D.M.S. Headqrs Rouen No 61/20/16 dated 6/2/16)	
14. 2. 16 BERTRANCOURT.	Routine Work. Inspection of Smoke Helmets.	
15. 2. 16. BERTRANCOURT.	Routine Work. Inspection of Motor Ambulance drivers rifles.	
16. 2. 16. BERTRANCOURT.	"B" Section relieved "C" Section at Advanced Dressing Station at SAILLY. "C" Section returned to BERTRANCOURT – took over Hospital duties.	

Instructions regarding War Diaries and Intelligence Summaries are contained in F. S. Regs., Part II. and the Staff Manual respectively. Title pages will be prepared in manuscript.

WAR DIARY

or

~~INTELLIGENCE SUMMARY.~~

(Erase heading not required.)

Army Form C. 2118.

Hour, Date, Place	Summary of Events and Information	Remarks and references to Appendices
17.2.16. BERTRANCOURT.	Routine Work. Inspection of Smoke Helmets. The 1914 Pattern Infantry Equipment issued to all N.C.O's & men. This simplifies the carrying of the mess tin, & is much more practicable than the former way of wearing the great coat bandolier fashion, and clean shirt etc being embodied in it, or either carried in the oil sheet, worn on the belt.	
18.2.16. BERTRANCOURT.	Routine Work.	
19.2.16. BERTRANCOURT.	Routine Work.	
20.2.16. BERTRANCOURT.	Routine Work. Divine Service held for all available men.	
21.2.16. BERTRANCOURT.	Routine Work. Inspection of Smoke Helmets	
22.2.16. BERTRANCOURT.	Routine Work. Inspection of Motor Ambulance drivers rifles.	
23.2.16. BERTRANCOURT.	Routine Work. Inspection of Clothing by the Quartermaster.	
24.2.16. BERTRANCOURT.	Routine Work.	
25.2.16. BERTRANCOURT.	Routine Work.	

(73989) W4141—463. 400,000. 9/14. H.&J.Ltd. Forms/C. 2118/10.

Instructions regarding War Diaries and Intelligence Summaries are contained in F. S. Regs., Part II. and the Staff Manual respectively. Title pages will be prepared in manuscript.

WAR DIARY

or

~~INTELLIGENCE SUMMARY.~~

(Erase heading not required.)

Army Form C. 2118.

Hour, Date, Place	Summary of Events and Information	Remarks and references to Appendices
26.2.16. BERTRANCOURT.	Usual Routine Work. A detachment of ten men was sent to HEBUTERNE for duty in connection with the extension of the Dressing Station.	
27.2.16. BERTRANCOURT.	Usual Routine Work. Divine Service held.	
28.2.16. BERTRANCOURT.	Usual Routine Work. Inspection of Smoke Helmets.	
29.2.16 BERTRANCOURT.	Usual Routine Work. Inspection of M.T. A.S.C. drivers rifles. LIEUT GODFREY RUSSELL-POTTER reported his arrival & taken on the strength. Two rooms were secured in a farm-house opposite the Hospital, & were utilised as a Dental Department, extractions, and repairs to dentures etc, fillings being done. This work greatly helps to keep the wastage of the Division to normal, as it prevents men being evacuated to Base for minor repairs.	

LIEUT. COL. R.A.M.C.T.
COMMANDING, 1st S.M.F. AMBULANCE.
(Imperial Service Unit.)

(73989) W4141—463. 400,000. 9/14. H.&J.Ltd. Forms/C. 2118/10.

48th Div

1/1 S.M. Field Ambulance

March 1916

March 1916

Instructions regarding War Diaries and Intelligence Summaries are contained in F. S. Regs., Part II. and the Staff Manual respectively. Title Pages will be prepared in manuscript.

WAR DIARY
or
INTELLIGENCE SUMMARY
(Erase heading not required.)

1/1st S.M. Fd Ambulance

Army Form C. 2118.

48

Vol 12

Place	Date	Hour	Summary of Events and Information	Remarks and references to Appendices
BERTRANCOURT	1.3.16		Usual Routine Work in Connection with Hospital + Collection of Sick And Wounded from COLINCAMPS.	
BERTRANCOURT	2.3.16		Usual Routine Work. Inspection of Smoke Helmets.	
BERTRANCOURT	3.3.16		Received order to move. General fatigues in Connection with Closing down Hospital.	
BERTRANCOURT	4.3.16		5 am Reveille 6.30 am Breakfast. 9 am Unit proceeded by March Route to BUS. Hospital opened up. Corrugated Iron + Canvas shelter being utilised as Wards, Dressing Room + Pack store etc.	
BUS	5.3.16		General fatigues in Connection with opening up Hospital. General Sanitation of Billeting Area Carried out. Divine Service held for all available men. Sick + Wounded were collected from areas allotted for A.D.M.S. 48th Divn. also from the Advanced Dressing Stations at COLINCAMPS, LA SUCRERIE + HEBUTERNE. These Advanced Dressing Stations being in Charge of Officers + men of this unit.	
BUS	6.3.16		General Routine Work in Connection with Hospital And	

2449 Wt. W14957/M90 750,000 1/16 J.B.C. & A. Forms/C.2118/12.

Instructions regarding War Diaries and Intelligence Summaries are contained in F. S. Regs., Part II. and the Staff Manual respectively. Title Pages will be prepared in manuscript.

WAR DIARY
or
INTELLIGENCE SUMMARY
(Erase heading not required.)

Army Form C. 2118.

Place	Date	Hour	Summary of Events and Information	Remarks and references to Appendices
Bus.	6.3.16		Advanced Dressing Stations. Order received from A.D.M.S. 48th Div. that only sick & wounded from our own Advanced Dressing Stations were to be treated in the Hospital.	
Bus.	7.3.16		General Routine Work. Inspection of Brit. A.S.C. drivers rifles.	
Bus.	8.3.16		General Routine Work. Inspection of Clothing by Quartermaster.	
Bus.	9.3.16		General Routine Work and Fatigues.	
Bus.	10.3.16		General Routine Work and Fatigues. Inspection of Brit. A.S.C. drivers rifles.	
Bus.	11.3.16		Routine Work & Fatigues.	
Bus.	12.3.16		Routine Work & Fatigues. Lecture given on the benefit and also necessity of Anti-Typhoid inoculation. The R.A.M.C. men doing transport duties were officially transferred to the A.S.C. (T)	
Bus.	13.3.16		Routine Work & Fatigues. Inspection of Smoke Helmets.	
Bus.	14.3.16		Routine Work & Fatigues. Inspection of Brit. A.S.C. drivers rifles.	

2449 Wt. W14957/M90 750,000 1/16 J.B.C. & A. Forms/C.2118/12.

Instructions regarding War Diaries and Intelligence Summaries are contained in F. S. Regs., Part II. and the Staff Manual respectively. Title Pages will be prepared in manuscript.

WAR DIARY
or
INTELLIGENCE SUMMARY
(Erase heading not required.)

Army Form C. 2118.

Place	Date	Hour	Summary of Events and Information	Remarks and references to Appendices
BUS.	15.3.16		Routine Work + fatigues. Inspection of Clothing by the Quartermaster.	
BUS.	16.3.16		Routine Work + fatigues. Inspection of ~~[illegible]~~ Smoke Helmets	
BUS.	17.3.16		Routine Work + fatigues. Inspection of Dr. & A.S.C. drivers rifles.	
BUS.	18.3.16		Routine Work + fatigues.	
BUS.	19.3.16		Routine Work + fatigues. The Officer + other ranks in charge of the Advanced Dressing Station at COLINCAMPS returned to Headquarters, being relieved by a detachment of the 1/2nd South Midland Field Ambulance.	
BUS.	20.3.16		Routine Work + fatigues. Inspection of Smoke Helmets.	
BUS.	21.3.16		Routine Work + fatigues. Inspection of Dr. & A.S.C. and H.T. A.S.C. drivers rifles.	
BUS.	22.3.16		Routine Work + fatigues. Inspection of Clothing by the Quartermaster.	

2449 Wt. W14957/M90 750,000 1/16 J.B.C. & A. Forms/C.2118/12.

Instructions regarding War Diaries and Intelligence Summaries are contained in F. S. Regs., Part II. and the Staff Manual respectively. Title Pages will be prepared in manuscript.

WAR DIARY or INTELLIGENCE SUMMARY

(Erase heading not required.)

Army Form C. 2118.

Place	Date	Hour	Summary of Events and Information	Remarks and references to Appendices
BUS.	2?.2.16.		Routine Work & Fatigues. The Advanced Dressing Station at "SAILLY" was taken over from us by the 1/2nd South Midland Field Ambulance.	
BUS.	2?.2.16		Routine Work & Fatigues. Inspection of R.A.M.C. and A.S.C. drivers rifles.	
BUS.	2?.2.16		Routine Work & Fatigues. LIEUT LOUIS JOSEPH LEGRIS reported his arrival for duty and was taken on the strength of the unit.	
BUS.	2?.2.16		Routine Work & Fatigues. Divine Service held for all available men.	
BUS.	2?.2.16		Routine Work & Fatigues. Inspection of Smoke Helmets.	
BUS.	28.2.16		Routine Work & Fatigues.	
BUS.	29.2.16		Routine Work & Fatigues. Inspection of Clothing by the Quartermaster. Inspection of Horse Transport by Commanding Officer.	
BUS.	2?.2.16		Routine Work & Fatigues. Inspection of Smoke Helmets.	

2449 Wt. W14957/M90 750,000 1/16 J.B.C. & A. Forms/C.2118/12.

Instructions regarding War Diaries and Intelligence Summaries are contained in F. S. Regs., Part II. and the Staff Manual respectively. Title Pages will be prepared in manuscript.

WAR DIARY
or
INTELLIGENCE SUMMARY
(Erase heading not required.)

Army Form C. 2118.

Place	Date	Hour	Summary of Events and Information	Remarks and references to Appendices
[illegible]	3.2.16		Routine Work & Fatigues. Received orders to Close down the Hospital, and be prepared to move at short notice. Arrangements made Accordingly. During the time the unit was in Charge of the Hospital, no Special Cases of wounds were received. There were Several Cases of German Measles Amongst the men of the Unit. Precautions were taken and no epidemic occurred. The prevailing diseases were Chiefly influenza, bronchitis & myalgia, the weather at this period being very cold.	

[illegible signature]
Major Comdg.
1st [illegible] Fd Ambulance

2449 Wt. W14957/M90 750,000 1/16 J.B.C. & A. Forms/C.2118/12.

April 1916.

1/1st S. Midland F. Amb.

Army Form C. 2118.

Instructions regarding War Diaries and Intelligence Summaries are contained in F. S. Regs., Part II. and the Staff Manual respectively. Title pages will be prepared in manuscript.

WAR DIARY
or
INTELLIGENCE SUMMARY.

(*Erase heading not required.*)

Hour, Date, Place	Summary of Events and Information	Remarks and references to Appendices
1. 4. 1916. SOUASTRE.	Unit moved from BUS and relieved 2nd L. Dn. Fld Ambulance. took over Hospital for sick and wounded – also baths for the treatment of scabies.	
2. 4. 1916 SOUASTRE	General fatigues Church Service.	
3 4 1916 SOUASTRE	Routine Work. Inspection of Smoke Helmets General fatigues in connection with the Hospital.	
4. 4. 1916 SOUASTRE	Routine Work + fatigues. Inspection of A.S.C. rifles. Inspection of Transport.	
5. 4. 1916 SOUASTRE.	Routine Work + fatigues. Baths were opened in a suitable barn, in the village and clean changes of clothing issued. Inspection of clothing by Quartermaster.	
6. 4. 16. SOUASTRE	Routine Work + fatigues. Inspection of Smoke Helmets by O.C. Sections.	
7. 4. 16. SOUASTRE	Routine Work + fatigues	
8. 4. 16. SOUASTRE	Routine Work + fatigues	
9. 4. 16. SOUASTRE	Routine Work. Church Service	
10. 4. 16. SOUASTRE	Routine Work. Inspection of Smoke Helmets. Lecture by the O. Comdg to the N.C.O's on discipline.	
11. 4. 16. SOUASTRE	Routine Work. Inspection of Rifles of the A.S.C. men attached.	

(73989) W4141—463. 400,000. 9/14. H.&J.Ltd. Forms/C. 2118/10.

Instructions regarding War Diaries and Intelligence Summaries are contained in F. S. Regs., Part II. and the Staff Manual respectively. Title pages will be prepared in manuscript.

WAR DIARY
or
~~INTELLIGENCE SUMMARY~~.
(Erase heading not required.)

Army Form C. 2118.

Hour, Date, Place		Summary of Events and Information	Remarks and references to Appendices
12. 4. 16.	SOUASTRE	Routine Work + Fatigues. Inspection of Smoke Helmets.	
13. 4. 16.	SOUASTRE	Routine Work + Fatigues	
14. 4. 16.	SOUASTRE	Routine Work + Fatigues. Lieut J. B. Butler transferred to 2nd/1st Ldn Field Ambulance for duty. Lieut D. G. Dobson reported his arrival for duty from No 4 General Hospital.	
15. 4. 16	SOUASTRE	Routine Work + Fatigues	
16. 4. 16.	SOUASTRE.	Routine Work. Church Services.	
17. 4. 16.	SOUASTRE	Routine Work. Inspection of Smoke Helmets. Inspection of Iron Rations	
18. 4. 16.	SOUASTRE	Routine Work. Inspection of rifles of A.S.C. men attached. Capt. F. J. Boome reported for duty from England.	
19. 4. 16.	SOUASTRE	Routine Work. Inspection of Clothing by Quartermaster.	
20. 4. 16.	SOUASTRE	Routine Work. Inspection of Smoke Helmets.	
21. 4. 16.	SOUASTRE	Routine Work + Fatigues	
22. 4. 16.	SOUASTRE	Routine Work + Fatigues	
23. 4. 16.	SOUASTRE	Routine Work + Fatigues	
24. 4. 16.	SOUASTRE	Routine Work + Fatigues. Inspection of Smoke Helmets.	
25. 4. 16.	SOUASTRE	Routine Work. Inspection of A.S.C. rifles.	

(73989) W4141—463. 400,000. 9/14. H.&J.Ltd. Forms/C. 2118/10.

Instructions regarding War Diaries and Intelligence Summaries are contained in F. S. Regs., Part II. and the Staff Manual respectively. Title pages will be prepared in manuscript.

WAR DIARY
or
~~INTELLIGENCE SUMMARY.~~
(Erase heading not required.)

Army Form C. 2118.

Hour, Date, Place	Summary of Events and Information	Remarks and references to Appendices
26.4.16. SOUASTRE	Routine Work. Inspection of Clothing by Quartermaster. The 2nd L. Mid Fd Ambulance relieved us at the Advanced Dressing Station SAILLY.	
27.4.16. SOUASTRE	Routine Work. Inspection of Smoke Helmets	
28.4.16. SOUASTRE	Routine Work + Fatigues	
29.4.16. SOUASTRE	Routine Work + Fatigues	
30.4.16. SOUASTRE	Routine Work + Fatigues	
	Routine Work + Fatigues	
	A Section being in charge of the hospital, which consisted of shelters and tents, and general fatigues being performed to make additional accomodation, also a party of men where detailed daily for duty at SAILLY assisting in the construction of Dug Outs. The dental department was opened in a room in a Chateau, the remaining portion being occupied as officers billets + officers mess. Much good work has been performed by the Dental Dept + the sick wastage of dental patients considerably reduced.	[signature]

(73989) W4141—463. 400,000. 9/14. H.&J.Ltd. Forms/C. 2118/10.

48th Div.

May 1916.

1st. S. Mid. F. Amb.

1 SM 2a Amb

Vol 14

48

Instructions regarding War Diaries and Intelligence Summaries are contained in F. S. Regs., Part II. and the Staff Manual respectively. Title pages will be prepared in manuscript.

WAR DIARY
or
INTELLIGENCE SUMMARY.

(Erase heading not required.)

Army Form C. 2118.

Hour, Date, Place	Summary of Events and Information	Remarks and references to Appendices
1/5/16. SOUASTRE	Routine Work. Inspection of Smoke Helmets. Bathing Parade. Lieut D. R. Dobson transferred to 1/2nd Ulster Regiment for duty.	
2/5/16. SOUASTRE	Routine Work & General Fatigues	
3/5/16. SOUASTRE	Routine Work & General Fatigues	
4/5/16. SOUASTRE.	2.0 am Reveille, 3.0 am Breakfast, 4.0 a.m. Unit paraded in column of route (2 Horse Ambulances in rear). Haversack rations carried & also forage for horses. Unit moved off behind 168th Infantry Brigade to Beauval (BEAUVAL), arriving at the latter place at 11 a.m. Hospital formed as part of a factory, extra accommodation being made by pitching tents on a field in the immediate vicinity.	
5/5/16 BEAUVAL –	Routine Work & General Fatigues in connection with the hospital & the sanitation of the billets etc carried out. Baths were opened at GEZAINCOURT, about 3 kilos. from here. 1 officer & 20 men being in charge. 1 officer & 120 men were bathed every hand and clean underclothing	

(73989) W4141—463. 400,000. 9/14. H.&J.Ltd. Forms/C. 2118/10.

Instructions regarding War Diaries and Intelligence Summaries are contained in F. S. Regs., Part II. and the Staff Manual respectively. Title pages will be prepared in manuscript.

WAR DIARY
or
~~INTELLIGENCE SUMMARY.~~
(Erase heading not required.)

Army Form C. 2118.

Hour, Date, Place		Summary of Events and Information	Remarks and references to Appendices
5/5/16	BEAUVAL	issued periodically to the men. An open air Swimming Bath was also constructed by making a dam in the river, this has been utilised to a great extent by the troops in the district (143 Infantry Brigade).	
6/5/16	BEAUVAL	General fatigues, Routine Work, Lectures given to the men by their Section Officers.	
7/5/16	BEAUVAL	Routine Work. Divine Service held	
8/5/16	BEAUVAL	Routine Work. Inspection of Smoke Helmets. Captain S. J. BOOME transferred to South Midland Casualty Clearing Station AMIENS for duty.	
9.5.16	BEAUVAL	Routine Work. Inspection of rifles of the A.S.C. drivers ~~[illegible]~~. Water Duty and Nursing Orderlies Classes Commenced. An officer being detailed to lecture for about two hours daily.	
10.5.16	BEAUVAL	Routine Work. Inspection of Clothing by Quartermaster. Lectures given to Water Duty men & also the Nursing Orderlies	

(73989) W4141—463. 400,000. 9/14. H.&J.Ltd. Forms/C. 2118/10.

Instructions regarding War Diaries and Intelligence Summaries are contained in F. S. Regs., Part II. and the Staff Manual respectively. Title pages will be prepared in manuscript.

WAR DIARY

or

~~INTELLIGENCE SUMMARY.~~

(Erase heading not required.)

Army Form C. 2118.

Hour, Date, Place		Summary of Events and Information	Remarks and references to Appendices
11.5.16.	BEAUVAL	Routine Work. Inspection of Smoke Helmets	
12.5.16.	BEAUVAL	Routine Work. Inspection of rifles of the A.S.C. attached	
13.5.16.	BEAUVAL	Routine Work. Route March of 15 miles carried out. Marching Order.	
14.5.16.	BEAUVAL	Routine Work. Divine Service held.	
15.5.16.	BEAUVAL	Routine Work. Inspection of Smoke Helmets	
16.5.16.	BEAUVAL	Routine Work. Inspection of rifles of the A.S.C. attached.	
17.5.16.	BEAUVAL	Routine Work. & General fatigues	
18.5.16.	BEAUVAL	Routine Work. Inspection of iron Rations	
19.5.16.	BEAUVAL	Routine Work. Lecture given to Nursing Orderlies	
20.5.16.	BEAUVAL	Routine Work & fatigues	
21.5.16.	BEAUVAL	Routine Work, fatigues. Divine Service.	
22.5.16.	BEAUVAL	Routine Work. Inspection of Smoke Helmets by Section Officers.	

(73989) W4141—463. 400,000. 9/14. H.&J.Ltd. Forms/C. 2118/10.

Instructions regarding War Diaries and Intelligence Summaries are contained in F. S. Regs., Part II. and the Staff Manual respectively. Title pages will be prepared in manuscript.

WAR DIARY
or
~~INTELLIGENCE SUMMARY.~~
(Erase heading not required.)

Army Form C. 2118.

Hour, Date, Place	Summary of Events and Information	Remarks and references to Appendices
23.5.16. BEAUVAL	Routine Work. Inspection of rifles of the A.S.C. attached.	
24.5.16. BEAUVAL	Routine Work. Inspection of Clothing by Quartermaster	
25.5.16. BEAUVAL	Routine Work. Inspection of Smoke Helmets	
26.5.16. BEAUVAL	Routine Work. Captain B. B. Morgan R.A.M.C. transferred to 1 Div Casualty Clearing Station for permanent duty.	
27.5.16. BEAUVAL	Routine Work. Fatigues.	
28.5.16. BEAUVAL	Routine Work. Divine Service held.	
29.5.16. BEAUVAL	Routine Work. Inspection of Smoke Helmets.	
30.5.16. BEAUVAL	Routine Work. Inspection of rifles of the A.S.C. attached.	
31.5.16. BEAUVAL	Routine Work. "C" Section moved with 145th Infantry Brigade to COULONVILLERS by [illegible] Route.	

(73989) W4141—463. 400,000. 9/14. H.&J.Ltd. Forms/C. 2118/10.

Instructions regarding War Diaries and Intelligence Summaries are contained in F. S. Regs., Part II. and the Staff Manual respectively. Title pages will be prepared in manuscript.

WAR DIARY
or
~~INTELLIGENCE SUMMARY.~~

(Erase heading not required.)

Army Form C. 2118.

Hour, Date, Place	Summary of Events and Information	Remarks and references to Appendices
	Route Marches were carried out as often as possible, with full marching order to enable the men to have training in this respect. The 1914 Pattern Infantry Equipment only recently being issued to the men. Physical drill was carried out.	
	C. Hawkins	

(73989) W4141—463. 400,000. 9/14. H.&J.Ltd. Forms/C. 2118/10.

June 1916

48th Division

1/1. S.M. Field Ambulance

June 1916

Vol June 1916

Instructions regarding War Diaries and Intelligence Summaries are contained in F. S. Regs., Part II. and the Staff Manual respectively. Title Pages will be prepared in manuscript.

WAR DIARY
or
INTELLIGENCE SUMMARY
(Erase heading not required.)

1/1st S. M. Field Ambulance.

Army Form C. 2118. 48

Vol 15

Place	Date	Hour	Summary of Events and Information	Remarks and references to Appendices
BEAUVAL	1.6.16	-	General Routine Work + Fatigues. Inspection of Smoke Helmets.	
"	2.6.16	-	General Routine Work + Fatigues. Inspection of the rifles of the A.S.C. Drivers.	
"	3.6.16	-	General Routine Work + Fatigues.	
"	4.6.16	-	Routine Work + Fatigues. "B" Section packed up and ready to move off with a Brigade of Infantry.	
"	5.6.16		Routine Work + Fatigues. Inspection of Smoke Helmets.	
"	5.6.16	3.30am	"B" Section moved off with 144th Infantry Brigade to the "Training Area" near Coulonvillers.	
"	6.6.16		Usual Routine Work + Fatigues. Inspection of the rifles of the A.S.C. drivers.	
"	7.6.16		Routine Work + Fatigues.	
"	8.6.16		Routine Work + Fatigues. Unit prepared to move by Draw... Route to HEM (A Section only). "B" + "C" Sections being in the Training Area with two Infantry Brigades.	

2449 Wt. W14957/M90 750,000 1/16 J.B.C. & A. Forms/C.2118/12.

Instructions regarding War Diaries and Intelligence Summaries are contained in F. S. Regs., Part II. and the Staff Manual respectively. Title Pages will be prepared in manuscript.

Army Form C. 2118.

WAR DIARY
or
INTELLIGENCE SUMMARY
(Erase heading not required.)

Place	Date	Hour	Summary of Events and Information	Remarks and references to Appendices
BEAUVAL	9.6.16		General fatigues, washing wagons, cleaning Hospital etc.	
		3 pm	"A" Section moved to HEM by [illegible] Route. 11th Field Ambulance relieved us at BEAUVAL.	
HEM.	10.6.16		Hospital formed, accomodation for patients being found by utilising barns. General fatigues in connection with the Hospital. Inspection of First Field Dressings.	
HEM	11.6.16		General Routine Work + Fatigues. Inspection of Iron Rations	
HEM	12.6.16		" " " " " . Inspection of Smoke Helmets	
HEM.	12.6.16		" " " " " Inspection of the rifles of the A.S.C. drivers.	
HEM	14.6.16		General Routine Work + Fatigues. Inspection of Clothing by the Quartermaster. "C" Section returned to Headquarters.	
HEM.	15.6.16		General Routine Work + Fatigues. "B" Section returned to Headquarters. The Unit prepared to move off at a moment's notice to relieve another Field Ambulance.	

2449 Wt. W14957/M90 750,000 1/16 J.B.C. & A. Forms/C.2118/12.

Instructions regarding War Diaries and Intelligence Summaries are contained in F. S. Regs., Part II. and the Staff Manual respectively. Title Pages will be prepared in manuscript.

WAR DIARY
or
INTELLIGENCE SUMMARY
(Erase heading not required.)

Army Form C. 2118.

Place	Date	Hour	Summary of Events and Information	Remarks and references to Appendices
HEM.	16.6.16	9 am.	Unit paraded in Full Marching Order and proceeded by March Route to ARQUEVES to be temporarily attached to the 29th Division for duty	
ARQUEVES	16.6.16	3 pm.	Arrived at ARQUEVES. Took over Hospital and Divisional Rest Station from 88th Field Ambulance.	
ARQUEVES	17.6.16		General Fatigues in Connection with the Hospital	
ARQUEVES	18.6.16		"A" Section in Charge of Hospital + Divisional Rest Station. The majority of the Cases for treatment being Scabies + other Skin troubles. "B" + "C" Sections held in reserve, ready to move off at a moment's notice	
ARQUEVES	19.6.16		General Routine Work. Fatigue parties for Cleaning and improving the hospital. Inspection of Iron Rations and Field Dressings, deficiencies made up.	
ARQUEVES	20.6.16		General Routine Work. Inspection of the Rifles of the Motor Ambulance + Horse transport drivers, rifles.	

2449 Wt. W14957/M90 750,000 1/16 J.B.C. & A. Forms/C.2118/12.

Instructions regarding War Diaries and Intelligence Summaries are contained in F. S. Regs., Part II. and the Staff Manual respectively. Title Pages will be prepared in manuscript.

Army Form C. 2118.

WAR DIARY
or
INTELLIGENCE SUMMARY
(Erase heading not required.)

Place	Date	Hour	Summary of Events and Information	Remarks and references to Appendices
ARQUEVES.	21.6.16		General Routine Work + Fatigues	
ARQUEVES.	22.6.16		do do do do	
ARQUEVES.	23.6.16		General Routine Work + Fatigues. A party for Train Duty consisting of 2 officers (Lieuts Legros + Potter) and 20 other ranks proceed to GEZAINCOURT for duty in conjunction with the 20th Casualty Clearing Station	
ARQUEVES.	24.6.16		General Routine Work + Fatigues	
ARQUEVES.	25.6.16		do do do do	
ARQUEVES.	26.6.16		General Routine Work + Fatigues. Inspection of Smoke Helmets.	
ARQUEVES.	27.6.16		General Routine Work + Fatigues	
ARQUEVES.	28.6.16		do do do do	
ARQUEVES.	29.6.16		do do do do. Inspection of Smoke Helmets.	
ARQUEVES.	30.6.16		Bearer Sub Divisions were attached to 88th Field Ambulance to assist in the collection of sick & wounded during the attack on	

2449 Wt. W14957/M90 750,000 1/16 J.B.C. & A. Forms/C.2118/12.

Instructions regarding War Diaries and Intelligence Summaries are contained in F. S. Regs., Part II. and the Staff Manual respectively. Title pages will be prepared in manuscript.

WAR DIARY
or
INTELLIGENCE SUMMARY.
(Erase heading not required.)

Army Form C. 2118.

Hour, Date, Place	Summary of Events and Information	Remarks and references to Appendices
ARQUEVES 20.6.16	BEAUMONT HAMEL One tent Sub. Division at MAILLY MAILLET to assist the 89th Field Ambulance	
	William McFall Major Comdg 1/2 1 Dr. Fld Ambulance	

(9 29 6) W2794 100,000 8/14 H W V Forms/C. 2118/11

July 1916

48th Div.

1/1st South Mid. Field Amb.

Instructions regarding War Diaries and Intelligence Summaries are contained in F. S. Regs., Part II. and the Staff Manual respectively. Title Pages will be prepared in manuscript.

WAR DIARY
or
~~INTELLIGENCE SUMMARY~~
(Erase heading not required.)

Army Form C. 2118.

1/1st Mid. Field Ambulance
Period 1.7.16 to 31.7.16

Place	Date	Hour	Summary of Events and Information	Remarks and references to Appendices
ARQUEVES	1.7.16	-	One Tent Sub Division running the 29th Divisional Rest Station & Sick Hospital at ARQUEVES. Two Bearer Sub-Divisions of the unit & one Tent Sub Division attached to the 88th Infantry Brigade 29th Division who were attacking BEAUMONT HAMEL. Details report attached hereto. Lt Col. J.H HOWKINS & CAPTAIN H.P. THOMASON were wounded by German Shrapnel whilst in charge of the Stretcher Squads who were working in the trenches.	
ARQUEVES	2.7.16		One Tent Sub Division under the Command of MAJOR H.F.W. BOEDDICKER returned from MAILLY-MALLET to the Headquarters at ARQUEVES. This Sub Division had been assisting the 88th Field Ambulance, and during the 24 hours ending midnight July 1st about 500 cases received medical attention there being sent to Hospital. Bearer Sub Divisions still working in the trenches at ENGLEBELMER. Major McCall [illegible] to ENGLEBELMER to take Command of the Stretcher Squads. Major BOEDDICKER in charge of Divisional Rest Station & Hospital at ARQUEVES.	
ARQUEVES	3.7.16	-	Routine Work in Connection with Divisional Rest Station and Hospital. Stretcher Squads still working in the trenches.	
ARQUEVES	4.7.16		Routine Work in Connection with Divisional Rest Station and Hospital	

2449 Wt. W14957/M90 750,000 1/16 J.B.C. & A. Forms/C.2118/12.

Instructions regarding War Diaries and Intelligence Summaries are contained in F. S. Regs., Part II. and the Staff Manual respectively. Title Pages will be prepared in manuscript.

WAR DIARY

or

~~INTELLIGENCE SUMMARY~~

(Erase heading not required.)

Army Form C. 2118.

Place	Date	Hour	Summary of Events and Information	Remarks and references to Appendices
ARQUEVES	4.7.16		The Bearer Sub. Divisions returned to Headquarters	
ARQUEVES	5.7.16		Routine Work in Connection with Divisional Rest Station & Hospital. Bearer Sub. Divisions resting in their Billets.	
ARQUEVES	6.7.16		Divisional Rest Station & Hospital work. This unit relieved the 48th Division ~~one~~ two parties ~~one~~ of 1 officer and 12 other ranks and 1 party of 1 N.C.O and 8 men proceeded to COLINCAMPS in charge of First Aid Station.	
ARQUEVES	7.7.16	10.0am	80th Field Ambulance took over Divisional Rest Station and Hospital. Two parties from COLINCAMPS returned to Headquarters. The Unit proceeded by march route to THIEVRES and held in reserve.	
THIEVRES	8.7.16		Reveille 6am. Parade 6.30am. Breakfast 7.30am. Parade 9 a.m. Kit inspection. 1pm Dinner. 2pm Parade. N.C.Os & men employed in overhauling & checking equipment. Cleaning wagons etc. a party of 1 N.C.O and 20 other ranks proceeded to HEBUTERNE to assist the 2nd/1st Div Fd Ambulance.	
THIEVRES	9.7.16		Parades as usual. General Fatigues. Inspection of Smoke Helmets. Church Parade for all available men.	
THIEVRES	10.7.16		Parades as usual. General Fatigues	
THIEVRES	11.7.16		Parades as usual. General Fatigues. Inspection of Dominion. Capt Rewater and 2 dental mechanics proceeded to 3rd Casualty [illegible]	

2449 Wt. W14957/M90 750,000 1/16 J.B.C. & A. Forms/C.2118/12.

Instructions regarding War Diaries and Intelligence Summaries are contained in F. S. Regs., Part II. and the Staff Manual respectively. Title Pages will be prepared in manuscript.

WAR DIARY

or

~~INTELLIGENCE SUMMARY~~

(Erase heading not required.)

Army Form C. 2118.

Place	Date	Hour	Summary of Events and Information	Remarks and references to Appendices
THIEVRES	11.7.16	–	Ambulance to open up a Dental Department	
THIEVRES	12.7.16		Parades + General Fatigues	
THIEVRES	13.7.16		Parades + Fatigues. Parties from HEBUTERNE + COLINCAMPS returned to Headquarters. One bearer sub-division and motor ambulances reported to D.D.M.S. X Corps for duty.	
THIEVRES	14.7.16		Unit proceeded by Route March to CONTAY	
CONTAY	15.7.16		Unit proceeded by Route March to BOUZINCOURT and took over from the 91st Field Ambulance 32. Division.	
BOUZINCOURT	16.7.16		The Headquarters + one Tent Sub Division were in charge of the Main Dressing Station at BOUZINCOURT. Three Bearer Sub Divisions and Tent Sub Division in charge of Aid Posts, the stretcher squads collecting the wounded + working in connection with the Regt. Medical Officers of the Infantry Battalions as far as possible.	
BOUZINCOURT	17.7.16		General Routine Work in connection with the Main Dressing Station + Advanced Dressing Stations. Inspection of Smoke Helmets of all Units.	
BOUZINCOURT	18.7.16		General Routine Work.	
BOUZINCOURT	19.7.16		A party of 2 officers and 19 other ranks proceeded to WARLOY to assist 1/2nd S. Mid. Fd Ambulance	

2449 Wt. W14957/M90 750,000 1/16 J.B.C. & A. Forms/C.2118/12.

Army Form C. 2118.

Instructions regarding War Diaries and Intelligence Summaries are contained in F. S. Regs., Part II. and the Staff Manual respectively. Title Pages will be prepared in manuscript.

WAR DIARY
or
~~INTELLIGENCE SUMMARY~~

(Erase heading not required.)

Place	Date	Hour	Summary of Events and Information	Remarks and references to Appendices
BOUZINCOURT	20.[illegible].16		Routine Work in connection with Main + Advanced Dressing Stations	
"	21.[illegible].16		do do do do do do do do do	
"	22.[illegible].16		do do do do do do do do do	
"	23.[illegible].16		do do do do do do do do do	
"	24.[illegible].16		do do do do do do do do do	
"	25.[illegible].16		do do do do do do do do do	
"	26.[illegible].16		The 2nd Field Ambulance 12th Division took over all Dressing Stations from us & the unit moved by March Route with the 145 Infantry Brigade to ARQUEVES. Bivouaced in the Open.	
ARQUEVES	27.[illegible].16		The unit resting awaiting further orders. An Inspection of clothing was held – the men were issued with new clothing as far as possible.	
ARQUEVES	28.[illegible].16		The unit moved by March Route with the 145 Infantry Brigade to BEAUVAL.	
BEAUVAL	29.[illegible].16		The unit moved by March Route with the 145 Infantry Brigade to DOMQUEUR. An Hospital was opened at DOMQUEUR for the reception of the sick of the Division. The Battalions being billeted in neighbouring villages.	
DOMQUEUR	30.[illegible].16		General Fatigues in connection with opening up Hospital	

2449 Wt. W14957/M90 750,000 1/16 J.B.C. & A. Forms/C.2118/12.

Army Form C. 2118.

WAR DIARY
or
INTELLIGENCE SUMMARY
(Erase heading not required.)

Instructions regarding War Diaries and Intelligence Summaries are contained in F. S. Regs., Part II. and the Staff Manual respectively. Title Pages will be prepared in manuscript.

Place	Date	Hour	Summary of Events and Information	Remarks and references to Appendices
DOMQUEUR	31.7.16		Routine Work and fatigues in Connection with hospital. Medical and Surgical equipment checked and overhauled. Wagons cleaned &c.	
			William McFall Major Commanding 1/2nd L. [illegible] Period 1.7.16 to 31.7.16	

2449 Wt. W14957/M90 750,000 1/16 J.B.C. & A. Forms/C.2118/12.

C O P Y

From The Officer Commanding,
1/1st South Midland Field Ambulance.

To The Assistant Director of Medical Services,
29th Division.

1st Southern General Hospital,
Edgbaston, Birmingham.
5th July 1916.

Report on 1st S.M.F.Ambulance on 1st July.

I regret that, on account of unavoidable circumstances, a consolidated report cannot be furnished in accordance with your operation order.

The following is what actually occurred as far as I was concerned.

The two bearer sub-divisions of the unit rested in the Redoubt Line between Gabion Avenue and Fort Moulin, on the night of Y.Z., and had orders not to move forward till the G.O.C. 88th Inf.Bde. sent them.

I visited the Redoubt Line at 9-30 a.m. and on my way passed several walking cases proceeding up Gabion Avenue to VITERMONT and on examination of several of them, I decided to establish a small "Rest Station" at the junction of the Redoubt Line with Gabion Avenue, so as to refix bandages, replace dressings, arrest haemorrhage, administer stimulants etc.,

All wounded who passed were examined, and if necessary treated.

This post did excellent work and was under Lieut. Davies-Jones and 2 orderlies.

Material to run it was obtained from the VITERMONT Dressing Station, so as to keep intact our bearers dressings etc.,

12-45 p.m. A message came from the G.O.C., 88th Inf. Bde. stating that there was a large number of wounded in the trenches.

Bearers were then taken up to the trenches occupied by the 88th Infantry Brigade, and a detachment lent to the M.O.i/c Knightsbridge Barracks to assist, as it was becoming congested.

After a reconnaissance and a visit to the Brigade Headquarters I decided to utilise all my bearers in clearing the trenches of wounded, and it was commenced under Capt. W. Bowater, O i/c Bearer Sub-Divisions.

The clearing proved very difficult and slow, the trenches being narrow, and frequently traversed.

The wounded to be cleared were the more serious class of cases and required careful handling.

5-20 p.m. I met the D.A.D.M.S., at VITERMONT and informed him of what I had seen and done.

6-30 p.m. On my return, near Knightsbridge, I met the bearers and Liaison Officer, who stated the G.O.C., 88th Brigade wished them to rest, and recommence at 10-0 p.m. when an Artillery Barrage would be formed.

The men then returned to the Redoubt Line, had tea and rested.

9-15 p.m. At 9-15 p.m. the bearer sub-divisions proceeded to Knightsbridge. Capt. W.Bowater took charge of one Bearer Sub-Division to first of all clear ~~kk~~ a Reg. Aid. Post (S.W.B.Regt.) in B.E.F. (or B) Street, which I had seen previously was clogged.

The Liaison Officer (Capt. Thomason) and I, with the other bearer sub-division proceeded towards the 88th Brigade Headquarters, so as to gain information as to where it could be best utilised to the greatest advantage.

The German Shrapnel was at this period very heavy, and a machine gun was playing over the trenches.

A Shrapnel shell burst over the trench through which we were passing and wounded Capt. Thomason 2 Bearers, and myself. The remaining bearers I placed under Capt Sanders, M.O.,1st Essex, to utilise to the best advantage.

A message reporting the matter was sent to you, Major McCall (second in command at 1st S.M.F.Amb, Headquarters, ARQUEVES) and a note for Capt. Bowater (O i/c Bearer Sub-Division) at

Knightsbridge.

I am unable to give ant further information as regards the further work of thw Unit.

The bearers worked well, Cheerfully and Bravely, although under great difficulties.

A tent Sub-Division was held in reserve at MAILLY-MAILLET and could have opened up at any time or place necessary.

COMMUNICATION. Besides the Liaison Officer and runners to work between Brigade Headquarters and Bearer Sub-Divisions, I kept an orderly at Knightsbridge to receive and transmit messages, and also had a Motor Cyclist at VITERMONT so that I could communicate to any place.

The Motor Cycle I placed also at the disposal of the O i/C Advanced Dressing Station, VITERMONT.

This system worked very well.

Aug. 1916.

1/1st S. M. F. A.

1/2nd S.M. Field Amb.

Army Form C. 2118.

WAR DIARY
or
~~INTELLIGENCE SUMMARY~~
(Erase heading not required.)

Instructions regarding War Diaries and Intelligence Summaries are contained in F. S. Regs., Part II. and the Staff Manual respectively. Title Pages will be prepared in manuscript.

1/1 SM 2nd Amb August 1916

Vol 17

Place	Date	Hour	Summary of Events and Information	Remarks and references to Appendices
DONQUER	1.8.16		Routine Work + fatigues in Connection with the Hospital	
DONQUER	2.8.16		Routine Work + fatigues in Connection with the Hospital. Medical + Surgical Equipment overhauled and checked, and deficiencies made up as far as possible.	
DONQUER	3.8.16		Usual Routine Work + fatigues. Inspection of Smoke Helmets.	
DONQUER	4.8.16		Usual Routine Work + fatigues	
DONQUER	5.8.16		Usual Routine Work + fatigues	
DONQUER	6.8.16		Routine Work + fatigues	
DONQUER	7.8.16		Routine Work + fatigues. Inspection of Smoke Helmets.	
DONQUER	8.8.16		Received orders to close down Hospital + be ready to move off at short notice. The necessary arrangements were made.	
DONQUER	9.8.16	1.30am	The Unit moved off in rear of 145th Infantry Brigade to BEAUVAL. Arrived at BEAUVAL at 3 p.m.	
BEAUVAL ~~[illegible]~~	10.8.16		5.15am. The Unit proceeded by March Route in rear of 145th Infantry Brigade to VARRENNES.	
VARRENNES	11.8.16		Personnel in the open fields in bivouacs. Unit resting pending further orders.	

2449 Wt. W14957/M90 750,000 1/16 J.B.C. & A. Forms/C.2118/12.

Instructions regarding War Diaries and Intelligence Summaries are contained in F. S. Regs., Part II. and the Staff Manual respectively. Title Pages will be prepared in manuscript.

WAR DIARY
or
INTELLIGENCE SUMMARY
(Erase heading not required.)

Army Form C. 2118.

Place	Date	Hour	Summary of Events and Information	Remarks and references to Appendices
VARRENNES	12.8.16		Received orders to proceed to BOUZINCOURT on 13.8.16 and relieve the 3rd Field Ambulance & take over Dressing Station at BOUZINCOURT and Advanced Posts at Crucifix Corner, OVILLERS, DONNETTS POST, BAPUME POST, NORTH CHIMNEY CORNER, ALBERT.	
VARRENNES	13.8.16	5.20 am	Proceeded by March Route to BOUZINCOURT and relieved the 3rd Field Ambulance. The relief was completed by 12 noon. One Bearer Sub-Division from the 1/2nd and 1/3rd South Midland Field Ambulances were attached to this Unit for duty as Stretcher Bearers.	
BOUZINCOURT	14.8.16		The Headquarters & one Tent Sub Division were in charge of the Main Dressing Station at BOUZINCOURT. The remainder of the Unit working at the various Aid Posts, collecting the wounded & working in connection with the Regimental Medical Officers.	
BOUZINCOURT	15.8.16		Routine Work in connection with the Main and Advanced Dressing Stations	
BOUZINCOURT	16.8.16		Routine Work in connection with the Main and Advanced Dressing Stations	

2449 Wt. W14957/M90 750,000 1/16 J.B.C. & A. Forms/C.2118/12.

Instructions regarding War Diaries and Intelligence Summaries are contained in F. S. Regs., Part II. and the Staff Manual respectively. Title Pages will be prepared in manuscript.

WAR DIARY
or
~~INTELLIGENCE SUMMARY~~
(Erase heading not required.)

Army Form C. 2118.

Place	Date	Hour	Summary of Events and Information	Remarks and references to Appendices
Bouzincourt	17.8.16		Routine Work + fatigues in Connection with Main and Advanced Dressing Stations.	
"	18.8.16		do do do	
"	19.8.16		do do do	
"	20.8.16		do do do	
"	21.8.16		do do do	
"	22.8.16		do do do	
"	23.8.16		do do do	
"	24.8.16		do do do	
"	25.8.16		do do do	
"	26.8.16		do do do	
"	27.8.16		The 1/1st Field Ambulance of the 25th Division relieved this Unit + took over all Dressing Stations and relieved the Stretcher Bearers.	
Bouzincourt	28.8.16		The unit proceeded to Bus and took over Hospital from 6th Field Ambulance. 2nd Division.	
Bus	29.8.16		General fatigues in Connection with the Hospital.	

2449 Wt. W14957/M90 750,000 1/16 J.B.C. & A. Forms/C.2118/12.

Instructions regarding War Diaries and Intelligence Summaries are contained in F. S. Regs., Part II. and the Staff Manual respectively. Title Pages will be prepared in manuscript.

WAR DIARY
or
INTELLIGENCE SUMMARY

(Erase heading not required.)

Army Form C. 2118.

Place	Date	Hour	Summary of Events and Information	Remarks and references to Appendices
Bus.	30.8.16	–	General Routine Work + Fatigues in Connection with the Hospital. Inspection of Clothing by Quartermaster.	
Bus.	31.8.16		Routine Work + Fatigues in Connection with the Hospital.	
			The Casualties of this Unit during the period at the Advanced Dressing Station:-	
			4 Wounded	
			3 Killed	

[illegible]
Major Comdg
[illegible] Field Ambulance

2449 Wt. W14957/M90 750,000 1/16 J.B.C. & A. Forms/C.2118/12.

Sept. 1916

48th Div

1/1st S. M. Field Ambulance

2nd/1st Midland Field Ambulance

WAR DIARY
or
INTELLIGENCE SUMMARY.
(Erase heading not required.)

September 1916

Army Form C. 2118.

Vol 18

Instructions regarding War Diaries and Intelligence Summaries are contained in F. S. Regs., Part II. and the Staff Manual respectively. Title pages will be prepared in manuscript.

Hour, Date, Place		Summary of Events and Information	Remarks and references to Appendices
1.9.16.	Bus.	General Routine Work in Connection with Hospital. Physical Drill & General training for all available men.	
2.9.16.	Bus.	General Routine Work & Fatigues. Inspection by G.O.C. of 48th Division	
~~[illegible]~~			
3.9.16.	Bus.	General Routine Work & Fatigues. Church Services held for the various denominations.	
4.9.16.	Bus.	General Routine Work & Fatigues in Connection with the Hospital. Lectures on Dressing & General Duties to all Sections.	
5.9.16.	Bus.	General Routine Work & Fatigues. Route Marches carried out by all available O.R's & Men.	
6.9.16.	Bus.	General Routine Work & Fatigues. Received orders to move to Sarton	

[illegible signature]

(73989) W4141—463. 400,000. 9/14. H.&J.Ltd. Forms/C. 2118/10.

Army Form C. 2118.

Instructions regarding War Diaries and Intelligence Summaries are contained in F. S. Regs., Part II. and the Staff Manual respectively. Title Pages will be prepared in manuscript.

WAR DIARY
or
~~INTELLIGENCE SUMMARY~~

(Erase heading not required.)

Place	Date	Hour	Summary of Events and Information	Remarks and references to Appendices
C.A.16 Bus	6.9.16	–	and open up an Hospital for the reception of sick from 143 Infantry Brigade. The 1/5th Royal Warwickshire Regiment was stationed at SARTON.	
C.A.16 Bus	7.9.16		~~General Routine Work~~ ~~Church Parade~~ ~~Fatigues~~ General Fatigues. Wagons packed. All patients remaining in Hospital were taken over by the 1/3rd S. Mid. Field Ambulance. The Unit proceeded by March Route to SARTON at 2 p.m.	
SARTON	8.9.16		General Fatigues in connection with the opening up of the Hospital.	
SARTON	9.9.16		General Routine Work & Fatigues. Route March carried out all available men paraded.	
SARTON	10.9.16		Routine Work. Church Parade.	
SARTON	11.9.16		Received orders to proceed by March Route with the 143 Infantry Brigade to GEZAINCOURT. Hospital closed down, moved off at 2 p.m. in rear of 143 Infantry Brigade.	
GEZAINCOURT	12.9.16		Unit in bivouacs in a field, hospital opened up for a small number of sick in a suitable barn.	
GEZAINCOURT	13.9.16		Routine Work & Fatigues. Lecture on [illegible] etc by Section Officers.	

2449 Wt. W14957/M90 750,000 1/16 J.B.C. & A. Forms/C.2118/12.

Instructions regarding War Diaries and Intelligence Summaries are contained in F. S. Regs., Part II. and the Staff Manual respectively. Title Pages will be prepared in manuscript.

WAR DIARY
or
~~INTELLIGENCE SUMMARY~~
(Erase heading not required.)

Army Form C. 2118.

Place	Date	Hour	Summary of Events and Information	Remarks and references to Appendices
BEZANCOURT	14.9.16		Routine Work + Fatigues. Route March carried out by all available men.	
BEZANCOURT	15.9.16		Routine Work + Fatigues. Lectures on various Medical Subjects by Section Officers.	
BEZANCOURT	16.9.16		Routine Work. During the period this Unit was Resting a Sports Committee was formed, and various races held in the afternoon. The Commanding Officer afterwards presented the prizes. The Corps Commander awarded the following N.C.O. & men, the Military Medal for Good work in the collection of sick & wounded during the period July 1st to July 3rd viz. Sgt. J. Garland. 1436 Pte. W. Elliott. 2012 Pte. W. J. Cox. 2205 Pte. Crecraft. 2001 Pte. F. C. Davey.	
BEZANCOURT	17.9.16		Routine Work. Church Parade. Orders received to close down Hospital & proceed by Route March with the 143 Infantry Brigade to a New Area, on 18.9.16.	
BEZANCOURT	18.9.16		5.30 a.m. Unit paraded, full Marching Order, and moved off in rear of 143rd Infantry Brigade. Unit arrived at ...	

2449 Wt. W14957/M90 750,000 1/16 J.B.C. & A. Forms/C.2118/12.

Instructions regarding War Diaries and Intelligence Summaries are contained in F. S. Regs., Part II. and the Staff Manual respectively. Title Pages will be prepared in manuscript.

WAR DIARY
or
~~INTELLIGENCE~~ SUMMARY

(Erase heading not required.)

Army Form C. 2118.

Place	Date	Hour	Summary of Events and Information	Remarks and references to Appendices
GEZAINCOURT	18.9.16		HILAIRE. A small hospital was opened up in a suitable house, additional accomodation being ~~formed~~ by Tents. Sick of the 143 Infantry Brigade collected and treated.	
S. HILAIRE	19.9.16		General fatigues, Inspection of Billets and General Sanitation Carried out. Water ~~[illegible]~~ Samples were taken from the various sources and found satisfactory	
St. HILAIRE	20.9.16		Routine Work + fatigues.	
S. HILAIRE	21.9.16		Routine Work, fatigues. Route Marches Carried out by all available N.C.Os + men.	
S. HILAIRE	22.9.16		Routine Work + fatigues, Captain W. BOWATER, awarded the Military Cross for Good work from the 1st July 1916.	
S. HILAIRE	23.9.16		Routine Work + fatigues. 6 pm. Hospital closed down. Unit moved by March Route to RIBEAUCOURT + BARLETTE.	
RIBEAUCOURT	24.9.16		General fatigues in Connection with the Hospital. A Dental Department was opened up at BARLETTE, Captain [illegible]	

2449 Wt. W14957/M90 750,000 1/16 J.B.C. & A. Forms/C.2118/12.

Instructions regarding War Diaries and Intelligence Summaries are contained in F. S. Regs., Part II. and the Staff Manual respectively. Title Pages will be prepared in manuscript.

WAR DIARY
or
~~INTELLIGENCE SUMMARY~~

(Erase heading not required.)

Army Form C. 2118.

Place	Date	Hour	Summary of Events and Information	Remarks and references to Appendices
RIBEAUCOURT	24.9.16		Bearers being in Charge.	
RIBEAUCOURT	25.9.16		General Routine Work + Fatigues	
RIBEAUCOURT	26.9.16		Routine Work in Connection with Hospital. All other Available Bearer N.C.O.s + men carried out a Route March ~~and~~ in Connection with a Divisional Scheme.	
RIBEAUCOURT	27.9.16		Routine Work + Fatigues. Route March carried out by all available N.C.O.s + men.	
RIBEAUCOURT	28.9.16		General Routine Work + Fatigues	
RIBEAUCOURT	29.9.16		Received orders to move to CANDAS. Hospital closed down all patients evacuated. 2 p.m. Proceeded by March Route to CANDAS.	
CANDAS	30.9.16		Received orders to move to HUMBERCOURT proceeded by March Route at 8 a.m. arrived at destination at 6 p.m.	

[illegible]
Capt Comdg
[illegible]

48th Divn

140/14/88

1/1 S M Field Ambulance

Oct 1916.

1st South Midland Fd Ambulance.

WAR DIARY
or
~~INTELLIGENCE SUMMARY~~

(Erase heading not required.)

October 1916

Army Form C. 2118.

1/1 SM Fd Amb

Vol 19

Instructions regarding War Diaries and Intelligence Summaries are contained in F. S. Regs., Part II. and the Staff Manual respectively. Title Pages will be prepared in manuscript.

Place	Date	Hour	Summary of Events and Information	Remarks and references to Appendices
HUMBERCAMPS	1.10.16		Received orders to proceed to St. AMAND & take over hospital at that place. Unit arrived at destination at 1 p.m. Lt. Col. C. H. Hawkins who was wounded on 1st July 1916 returned to Unit & assumed Command from 1.10.16.	
St. AMAND	2.10.16		General Routine Work & Fatigues in Connection with the hospital. A party of 1 Officer & 50 other ranks from "C" Section proceeded to take over the Advanced Dressing Station at FONQUEVILLERS from a Field Ambulance of the 40th Division. Inspection of Smoke Helmets by O.C. Sections.	
St. AMAND.	3.10.16		General Routine Work & Fatigues. Inspection of Identity Discs.	
St. AMAND.	4.10.16		Routine Work & Fatigues in connection hospital. Extra accomodation being made by erecting new shelter.	
St. AMAND.	5.10.16		Routine Work & Fatigues.	
St. AMAND.	6.10.16		Routine Work & Fatigues. Inspection of Smoke Helmets by O.C. Sections	
St. AMAND	7.10.16		Routine Work & Fatigues.	
St. AMAND	8.10.16		Routine Work & Fatigues. Divine Service for the various denominations	
St. AMAND	9.10.16		Routine Work & Fatigues. Improvements to the hospital still in course of erection.	
St. AMAND	10.10.16		Routine Work & Fatigues. Extra accomodation being provided & arrangements made in the event of the present hospital being utilised either as a Divisional or Corps Collecting Station.	

2449 Wt. W14957/M90 750,000 1/16 J.B.C. & A. Forms/C.2118/12.

Instructions regarding War Diaries and Intelligence Summaries are contained in F. S. Regs., Part II. and the Staff Manual respectively. Title Pages will be prepared in manuscript.

WAR DIARY
or
~~INTELLIGENCE SUMMARY~~
(Erase heading not required.)

Army Form C. 2118.

Place	Date	Hour	Summary of Events and Information	Remarks and references to Appendices
St. AMAND	11.10.16		Routine Work & Fatigues in Connection with the hospital and also to improve & enlarge the existing accomodation.	
St. AMAND	12.10.16		Routine Work & Fatigues. Inspection of Smoke Helmets.	
St. AMAND	13.10.16		Routine Work & Fatigues. Water Carts overhauled by the Water Duty men & inspected by an Officer of this Unit.	
St. AMAND	14.10.16		Routine Work & Fatigues as usual.	
St. AMAND	15.10.16		Routine Work & Fatigues. Divine Services held for the various denominations.	
St. AMAND	16.10.16		Routine Work & Fatigues. The enlargement of the hospital being practically completed.	
St. AMAND	17.10.16		Routine Work & Fatigues. Inspection of Smoke Helmets by O.C. Sections.	
St. AMAND	18.10.16		Routine Work & Fatigues in Connection with hospital.	
St. AMAND	19.10.16		Routine Work, Fatigues etc.	
St. AMAND	20.10.16		Routine Work & Fatigues. Received orders to be prepared to move at a moments notice. The necessary arrangements were therefore made. The Unit moved by Road Route to GRAND RULLECOURT, arrived at destination at 1.30 p.m. Hospital opened up for the reception of sick. The personnel were billeted in large rooms & Canvas huts. Also several of the huts were utilised for wards. Tents being pitched for any extra accomodation.	

2449 Wt. W14957/M90 750,000 1/16 J.B.C. & A. Forms/C.2118/12.

Instructions regarding War Diaries and Intelligence Summaries are contained in F. S. Regs., Part II. and the Staff Manual respectively. Title Pages will be prepared in manuscript.

WAR DIARY
or
~~INTELLIGENCE SUMMARY~~
(Erase heading not required.)

Army Form C. 2118.

Place	Date	Hour	Summary of Events and Information	Remarks and references to Appendices
GRAND RULLECOURT	21.10.16	–	Routine Work + Fatigues in Connection with hospital. Baths were opened + were utilised by the 143rd Infantry Brigade. Men from the personnel of this Unit being in Charge of the Baths. These Baths were already built + had evidently been there for some time. They were of the "Spray" System.	
GRAND RULLECOURT	22.10.16		Routine Work + Fatigues. Inspection of Clothing by the Quartermaster.	
GRAND RULLECOURT	23.10.16		General Routine Work + Fatigues. Inspection of Smoke Helmets by O.C. Section.	
GRAND RULLECOURT	24.10.16		Received orders to move to FRANVILLER. The mounted Section of the Unit proceeding by March Route with the transport of the 142nd Infantry Brigade. The remainder of the Unit remained behind, being moved on the 25.10.16 by Motor lorries in conjunction with the 142 Infantry Brigade.	
GRAND RULLECOURT	25.10.16		The unit paraded in Full Marching Order at 10.45 a.m. + moved off at 10.55. Entered the motor buses at 12.15 p.m. on the E side of the SAULTY-SOMBRIN road. Arrived at FRANVILLER at [illegible] Billeted for the night in Barns + other farm buildings.	
FRANVILLER	26.10.16		The unit paraded at 8 a.m. in Full Marching Order + moved off at 8.20 a.m. arriving at MILLENCOURT at [illegible]. The Headquarter Section took over the hospital from the 2/3rd Northumbrian Field Ambulance. 2 officers + 3[illegible] other ranks of the unit were temporarily attached	

2449 Wt. W14957/M90 750,000 1/16 J.B.C. & A. Forms/C.2118/12.

Army Form C. 2118.

Instructions regarding War Diaries and Intelligence Summaries are contained in F. S. Regs., Part II. and the Staff Manual respectively. Title Pages will be prepared in manuscript.

WAR DIARY
or
~~INTELLIGENCE SUMMARY~~
(Erase heading not required.)

Place	Date	Hour	Summary of Events and Information	Remarks and references to Appendices
FRANVILLERS	26.10.16		on duty at BECOURT CHATEAU (No 1 Main Dressing Station) III Corps. One Bearer Sub Division proceeded to LAVIEVILLE & took over from South African Field Ambulance	
MILLENCOURT	27.10.16		General Routine Work & Fatigues in Connection with Hospital. Collection of Sick under arrangements ordered by the A.D.M.S.	
MILLENCOURT	28.10.16		General Routine Work & Fatigues	
MILLENCOURT	29.10.16		General Routine Work & Fatigues	
	30.10.16		General Routine Work & Fatigues	
MILLENCOURT	31.10.16		General Routine Work & Fatigues. Instruction in Smoke Helmets to the Sections.	

C. Hawkins

Lieut Col Officer Comdg
1/2 [illegible] Fd Amb

2449 Wt. W14957/M90 750,000 1/16 J.B.C. & A. Forms/C.2118/12.

Nov. 1916

48th Div.

140/849

Army Form C. 2118.

Instructions regarding War Diaries and Intelligence Summaries are contained in F. S. Regs., Part II. and the Staff Manual respectively. Title pages will be prepared in manuscript.

WAR DIARY
or
INTELLIGENCE SUMMARY.

(Erase heading not required.)

Vol 20

Hour, Date, Place	Summary of Events and Information	Remarks and references to Appendices
	1/1st South Midland Field Ambulance	
	From 1st November 1916 to 30 November 1916.	

(73989) W4141—463. 400,000. 9/14. H.&J.Ltd. Forms/C. 2118/10.

Instructions regarding War Diaries and Intelligence Summaries are contained in F. S. Regs., Part II. and the Staff Manual respectively. Title Pages will be prepared in manuscript.

WAR DIARY
or
INTELLIGENCE SUMMARY

(Erase heading not required.)

Army Form C. 2118.

Place	Date	Hour	Summary of Events and Information	Remarks and references to Appendices
MILLENCOURT	1.11.16.		General Routine Work & fatigues in connection with the Hospital. Each N.C.O. & man received his first issue of Steel helmet.	
MILLENCOURT	2.11.16		Received orders to take over Advanced Dressing Station at CONTALMAISON CHATEAU and MARTINPUICH and other Advanced Posts from the [illegible] Field Ambulance 50th Division. The Bearer Sub Divisions of A, B & C Sections moved off at 9.0 am to take over from the [illegible] Field Ambulance.	
MILLENCOURT	3.11.16.	9am	The remainder of the Unit proceeded by March Route to CONTALMAISON & took over Advanced Dressing Stations at CONTALMAISON and MARTINPUICH, move completed & all details carried out by 12 noon. The Headquarters of the Unit was situated at CONTALMAISON CHATEAU which was recently captured by us from the enemy, the whole of the building being practically demolished to the ground, only the ground floor remaining & the basement or cellars. Underneath the latter the enemy had dug very good dug-outs which were utilised by us as sleeping accommodation for the officers & other ranks & also as officers mess. The depth would be about 30 ft from ground level. The Basement had three rooms, one being utilised as Dressing Room for wounded & the other as Waiting Room & Medical Stores, the rooms on the Ground Floor being used as Waiting & Reception Rooms for Morning sick & also sick from the trenches, also as Stores. Bearers from the 1/2nd & 1/3rd South Midland Field Ambulances were sent to assist. All wounded lying cases were hand carried to the Advanced Dressing Station at MARTINPUICH where they received medical attention & from thence carried to trollies (worked on rails pushed by hand) & pushed to VILLA POST a distance of about	

2449 Wt. W14957/M90 750,000 1/16 J.B.C. & A. Forms/C.2118/12.

Army Form C. 2118.

Instructions regarding War Diaries and Intelligence Summaries are contained in F. S. Regs., Part II. and the Staff Manual respectively. Title Pages will be prepared in manuscript.

WAR DIARY
or
INTELLIGENCE SUMMARY
(Erase heading not required.)

Place	Date	Hour	Summary of Events and Information	Remarks and references to Appendices
	3.11.16	–	one mile (a Horse Ambulance is always stationed here) & then they are carried to the Headquarters Advanced Dressing Station where they are redressed if necessary. The distance from VILLA POST to CONTALMAISON is about 1 mile. A supply of hot soup & tea is kept ready night & day & each patient has a meal before being sent from Headquarters. The patients are then evacuated by Motor Ambulance to Casualty Clearing Stations etc.	
CONTALMAISON	4.11.16.		Routine Work & carriage of wounded as described above. General fatigues in connection with the improvement of the area, paths made and shell holes filled in, & doors etc put up in the Chateau where necessary. Debris cleared away, & the area generally improved	
CONTALMAISON	5.11.16		Fatigues & Routine Work as above mentioned.	
– do –	6.11.16		do do do do	
– do –	7.11.16		do do do do	
– do –	8.11.16		do do do do	
– do –	9.11.16		do do do do CAPT. W. BOWATER is struck off the strength having been evacuated to England sick. LIEUT. [illegible] EDWARDS (R.A.) having reported has arrived & taken on the strength.	
CONTALMAISON	10.11.16		Fatigues & Routine Work	
do	11.11.16		do do do	
do	12.11.16		do do do.	
do	13.11.16		do do do. A relief of 20 Stretcher bearers carried out.	
do	14.11.16		do do do	
do	15.11.16		do do do	
do	16.11.16		do do do The Tent Sub Division in charge of Advanced Dressing Station at MARTINPUICH were relieved by the Tent Sub Division [illegible]	
do	17.11.16		Fatigues & Routine Work	
do	18.11.16		do do do.	

2449 Wt. W14957/M90 750,000 1/16 J.B.C. & A. Forms/C.2118/12.

WAR DIARY
or
INTELLIGENCE SUMMARY

(Erase heading not required.)

Army Form C. 2118.

Instructions regarding War Diaries and Intelligence Summaries are contained in F. S. Regs., Part II. and the Staff Manual respectively. Title Pages will be prepared in manuscript.

Place	Date	Hour	Summary of Events and Information	Remarks and references to Appendices
CONTALMAISON	19.11.16		Fatigues & Routine Work.	
– do –	20.11.16		do do do	
– do –	21.11.16		do do do	
– do –	22.11.16		do do do	
– do –	23.11.16		do do do.	
– do –	24.11.16		do do do.	
– do –	25.11.16		do do do.	
– do –	26.11.16		do do do. Capt W. Bowater is taken on the strength of the unit, having reported his arrival from England.	
– do –	27.11.16		Fatigues & Routine Work.	
– do –	28.11.16		do do do	
– do –	29.11.16		do do do	
– do –	30.11.16		do do do	
			A Divisional Soup Kitchen was formed at VILLA POST. The various battalions subsidising bones + meat etc. Hot soup was always ready + was given to any person who cared to have it. It was a great benefit to the men coming out the trenches on being relieved + also by the incoming battalion.	
			The habitable part of the Chateau was renovated as much as possible + bathrooms made + erected to support wash huts. Paths were made where the principal traffic occurred, also standings for water carts, a new cookhouse was also erected. Covered standing was erected for about 20 horses, etc.	

C. Hawkins
LIEUT. COL. R.A.M.C.T.
COMMANDING, 1st S.M.F. AMBULANCE.

2449 Wt. W14957/M90 750,000 1/16 J.B.C. & A. Forms/C.2118/12.

Dec 1916

48th Division

140/900

1/1st S. M. Field Ambulance

Army Form C. 2118.

WAR DIARY
or
INTELLIGENCE SUMMARY
(Erase heading not required.)

Instructions regarding War Diaries and Intelligence Summaries are contained in F. S. Regs., Part II. and the Staff Manual respectively. Title Pages will be prepared in manuscript.

Vol 21

Place	Date	Hour	Summary of Events and Information	Remarks and references to Appendices
			1/1st South Midland Field Ambulance.	
			1st Dec. 1916 to 31. Dec. 1916.	

2449 Wt. W14957/M90 750,000 1/16 J.B.C. & A. Forms/C.2118/12.

Army Form C. 2118.

Instructions regarding War Diaries and Intelligence Summaries are contained in F. S. Regs., Part II. and the Staff Manual respectively. Title Pages will be prepared in manuscript.

WAR DIARY
or
INTELLIGENCE SUMMARY
(Erase heading not required.)

Place	Date	Hour	Summary of Events and Information	Remarks and references to Appendices
CONTALMAISON	1.12.16		General Routine Work + fatigues in connection with the Advanced Dressing Station, improvement of area occupied by erecting Nissen + Amiens Huts for accomodation by officers and other ranks. Stabling erected for Horses. The following reinforcements reported their arrival and were taken on the strength 2059 Pte. R. J. Hopkins, 1928 Pte. J. Howard, 2020 Pte. H. W. England, 2387 Pte. W. Stanley	
CONTALMAISON	2.12.16.		General Routine Work + fatigues. Reliefs were carried out by the Bearer Sub-Divisions at rest + those working the line from the Advanced Dressing Stations. All ranks were warned to see that their iron rations are complete + in good condition as they may have to be consumed in lieu of a days rations	
CONTALMAISON	3.12.16.		General Routine Work + fatigues. Divine Services held.	
CONTALMAISON	4.12.16		— do — do —	
— do —	5.12.16		— do — do	
do	6.12.16		do. do	
do	7.12.16		do. do	
do	8.12.16		do do	
do	9.12.16		do do	
do	10.12.16		do do	
do	11.12.16		do do	
do	12.12.16		General Routine Work + fatigues. Iron Rations were consumed in lieu of ordinary rations.	
do.	13.12.16		General Routine Work + fatigues.	
do	14.12.16		do. do. do.	
do	15.12.16.		Received orders to move. One Tent Sub-Division proceeded to BAISIEUX and relieved a Section of the 45th Field Ambulance. Hospitals and Billets taken over. Reliefs carried out as far as possible at Adv. Dressing Station.	
do	16.12.16.		Relief carried out + completed by the 45th Field Ambulance. Unit proceeded by Draven Route to BAISIEUX and took over hospital and billets formerly occupied by the 45th Field Ambulance.	

2449 Wt. W14957/M90 750,000 1/16 J.B.C. & A. Forms/C.2118/12.

Instructions regarding War Diaries and Intelligence Summaries are contained in F. S. Regs., Part II. and the Staff Manual respectively. Title Pages will be prepared in manuscript.

WAR DIARY
or
INTELLIGENCE SUMMARY
(Erase heading not required.)

Army Form C. 2118.

Place	Date	Hour	Summary of Events and Information	Remarks and references to Appendices
CONTALMAISON	16.12.16	—	One Section proceeded to ALBERT and took over hospital from 46th Field Ambulance.	
BAIZIEUX	17.12.16		Routine Work in Connection with the Hospital. Equipment + stores were checked + overhauled.	
BAIZIEUX	18.12.16		Routine Work. Inspection of Smoke Helmets. The Unit at this time being at rest all working parties commenced at 9 a m and finished at 2. p. m thus giving them the remainder of the day for recreation purposes, they had an interval of 15 minutes at 11.30 a.m for lunch.	
BAIZIEUX	19.12.16.		Routine Work. Fatigues for Harness Cleaning. Wagon Cleaning. etc. Not many patients were coming to Hospital.	
BAIZIEUX	20.12.16.		General Routine Work + Fatigues	
BAIZIEUX	21.12.16		General Routine Work + Fatigue	
BAIZIEUX.	22.12.16		— do — — do — — do — — do —	
BAIZIEUX	23.12.16		— do — — do — — do — — do —	
BAIZIEUX	24.12.16		— do — — do — — do — — do —	
BAIZIEUX	25.12.16		Divine Services for various denominations. Sufficient accommodation was available in the billets, + was utilised as Mess Rooms for the Men. Xmas Dinner etc was given to the personnel at 2. p.m.	
BAIZIEUX	26.12.16		General Routine Work + Fatigues.	
BAIZIEUX	27.12.16		Preparations were made to close down the Hospital. Wagons packed etc.	
BAIZIEUX	[illegible]		One Section proceeded to BECOURT CHATEAU to relieve a Section of the 46th Fld Amb.	
BAIZIEUX	[illegible]		Unit proceeded by Brown Route to BECOURT CHATEAU and took over No 1 Main Dressing Station from 46th Field Ambce.	
BECOURT CHATEAU }	29.12.16		"A" Section in Charge of Reception Room. Operating Theatre. "C" Section in Charge of Hospital Marquees + Evacuation. "B" Section in readiness to take over No 2 Main Dressing Station.	
— do —	30.12.16		Routine Work. Fatigues for erecting Huts + improving the area etc	
— do —	31.12.16		"B" Section started relief with 1/3rd Northumbrian Fld Ambce at No 2 Main Dressing Station.	

C. Hawkins
Lieut Col. Officer Comdg
1/2nd S. Mn. Field Ambce.

2449 Wt. W14957/M90 750,000 1/16 J.B.C. & A. Forms/C.2118/12.

48th Div

Jan 1917 **Confidential.** 140/194/1 Vol 22

War Diary of

1/1st South Midland Field Ambulance.

48th Division. for period January 1st to 31st 1917.

Volume 22.

1/1st South Midland Field Ambulance

WAR DIARY
or
~~INTELLIGENCE SUMMARY~~

(Erase heading not required.)

January 1917

Army Form C. 2118.

Instructions regarding War Diaries and Intelligence Summaries are contained in F. S. Regs., Part II. and the Staff Manual respectively. Title Pages will be prepared in manuscript.

Place	Date	Hour	Summary of Events and Information	Remarks and references to Appendices
BECOURT	1.1.17		No. 1 Main + No 2 Main Dressing Station were formed into the III Corps Main Dressing under the Command of Lt Col C.H. Hawkins R.A.M.C. 2 officers and 56 other ranks of the 1st Field Ambulance 1st Division detailed for duty. The work here consisted chiefly of renovating the general accommodation. Trench boards being laid down, + these were covered by wire netting to improve the walking facilities when carrying patients, such as trench feet cases. The netting also saved the wear and tear of the boards. Trenches were filled in when possible. Dug-outs were made to accommodate personnel + patients in the event of hostile shelling, also trenches leading to existing dug-outs were improved. Nissens Huts were erected, being used as billets also as office. The principal medical work started at 2 p.m. when the Ambulance train arrived, the average number of patients being 200. The patients were then conveyed by R.A.M.C orderlies to the Reception Room, where hot tea + food was given to them. They then were seen by Medical Officers, redressed if necessary. An injection of A.T. Serum given where necessary. After being seen by the Medical Officer they were transferred to the Evacuation Tent to await the arrival of the Motor Ambulance Convoy at 6 p.m. All cases were then evacuated by the Convoy. Special cases were evacuated direct to C.C.S. if necessary.	
BECOURT	2.1.17		Usual Routine Work as above	
"	31.1.17		— do —	

2449 Wt. W14957/M90 750,000 1/16 J.B.C. & A. Forms/C.2118/12.

Army Form C. 2118.

Instructions regarding War Diaries and Intelligence Summaries are contained in F. S. Regs., Part II. and the Staff Manual respectively. Title Pages will be prepared in manuscript.

WAR DIARY
or
~~INTELLIGENCE SUMMARY~~
(Erase heading not required.)

Place	Date	Hour	Summary of Events and Information	Remarks and references to Appendices
BECOURT	4.1.19		General Routine Work & Fatigues	
"	5.1.19		– do – do – do – do –	
"	6.1.19		– do – do – do – do –	
"	7.1.19		– do – do – do – do. Divine Service Held.	
"	8.1.19		– do – do do do	
"	9.1.19		do do do do	
"	10.1.19		do do do do	
"	11.1.19		do do do do	
"	12.1.19		do do do do	
"	13.1.19		do do do do	
"	14.1.19		do do do do	
"	15.1.19		do do do do	
"	16.1.19		do do do do	
"	17.1.19		do do do do	
"	18.1.19		do do do do	
"	19.1.19		do do do do	
"	20.1.19		do do do do. Divine Service Held.	
"	21.1.19		do do do	
"	22.1.19		General Routine Work & Fatigues. Capt Brewster acting temporarily as [illegible]	

Instructions regarding War Diaries and Intelligence Summaries are contained in F. S. Regs., Part II. and the Staff Manual respectively. Title Pages will be prepared in manuscript.

WAR DIARY
or
~~INTELLIGENCE SUMMARY~~
(Erase heading not required.)

Army Form C. 2118.

Place	Date	Hour	Summary of Events and Information	Remarks and references to Appendices
BECOURT	23.1.17	—	General Routine Work + Fatigues. Detachments from No 1 Field Ambulance, 1st Division + 46. Field Amb-lce rejoined their own Units.	
BECOURT	24.1.17		General Routine Work + Fatigues	
"	25.1.17		——— do ———	
"	26.1.17		——— do ——— Tents and Marquees taken down preparatory to moving. All surplus stores dumped.	
"	27.1.17		The Unit, less Rear Party, left BECOURT at 9 am, and proceeded to MORCOURT, taking over the hospital and billets at the farm evacuated by the French in connection with the relief of the 152nd French Division by the 48th Division. Lieut Challons and 30 other ranks remained at BECOURT to take charge of the III Corps Medical Dump for surplus equipment.	
MORCOURT.	28.1.17		General Routine Work and Fatigues. Incinerator built, and rubbish collected & burnt.	
"	29.1.17		——— " ——— Various water supplies in the village tested, reports made and Area Commandant supplied with particulars.	
"	30.1.17		"A" Section opened Hospital to receive sick from 144th Brigade.	
"	31.1.17		General Routine Work in connection with Hospital.	

[signature]
Lieut-Col. R.A.M.C. T.
Officer Commanding 1/1st S. Mid Field Ambulance

Feb. 1917

48th Div.

140/1974

1/1st S. M. Field Ambulance

Appx 1 & 1^A —

Taken by [illegible] Chittenden

22-4 17 & filed

with Summary

1/1 S. M. F. A. Feb 1917

Instructions regarding War Diaries and Intelligence Summaries are contained in F. S. Regs., Part II. and the Staff Manual respectively. Title pages will be prepared in manuscript.

WAR DIARY
or
INTELLIGENCE SUMMARY.
(Erase heading not required.)

Army Form C. 2118.

48

Vol 24 3

Place	Date	Hour	Summary of Events and Information	Remarks and references to Appendices
			War Diary of 1st South Midland Field Ambulance Period 1.2.17 to 28.2.17.	

1577 Wt. W10791/1773 500,000 1/15 D. D. & L. A.D.S.S./Forms/C. 2118.

Instructions regarding War Diaries and Intelligence Summaries are contained in F. S. Regs., Part II. and the Staff Manual respectively. Title pages will be prepared in manuscript.

WAR DIARY
or
INTELLIGENCE SUMMARY.
(Erase heading not required.)

Army Form C. 2118.

Place	Date	Hour	Summary of Events and Information	Remarks and references to Appendices
MORCOURT.	1.2.17	-	General Routine Work + Fatigues	
MORCOURT.	2.2.17	-	Received Order to move to CAPPY. 6.0 a m Reveille. 6.30 a m Parade. Blankets rolled & loaded on Wagons. 7.0 a m Breakfast. 8.30 a m. Parade. Full Marching Order. Main Body and Transport moved off independently, arriving at CAPPY at 1 pm.	
CAPPY	3.2.17	-	6.30 a m Reveille. 7.30 a m. Breakfast. 9.0 a m. Inspection by Commanding Officer. General Fatigues pending order to open up Hospital. Captain Bowater returned from [illegible] Rest having been temporarily on detached duty.	
CAPPY	4.2.17		7.0 am. Reveille. 7.30 am Breakfast. 9.30 am Parade. 10.0 am. Church Service.	
CAPPY	5.2.17		6.30 am Reveille. 7.30 am. Breakfast. 9.0 am. Parade Inspection by Commanding Officer. 2.0 pm Parade. General Fatigues	
CAPPY	6.2.17		6.30 am Reveille. 7.30 am Breakfast. 9.0 am. Inspection by Commanding Officer. 1 Officer + 12 other ranks to [illegible]	

1577 Wt. W10791/1773 500,000 1/15 D. D. & L. A.D.S.S./Forms/C. 2118.

Instructions regarding War Diaries and Intelligence Summaries are contained in F. S. Regs., Part II. and the Staff Manual respectively. Title pages will be prepared in manuscript.

Army Form C. 2118.

WAR DIARY
or
INTELLIGENCE SUMMARY.
(Erase heading not required.)

Place	Date	Hour	Summary of Events and Information	Remarks and references to Appendices
LAPPY	6.2.15		to take over new billets, stabling etc adjoining LAPPY church. The Unit took over premises recently vacated by the French Ambulance. Fatigues carried out and Hospital prepared for the reception of sick + wounded.	
LAPPY	7.2.15		6.0 am Reveille 6.30 am Breakfast for Hospital Staff. 7.0 am Parade for Hospital Staff. 9.0 am Parade for remainder of Unit. Inspection by Commanding Officer. 2.0 pm Parade. General Fatigues in improving sleeping accomodation also improving the Hospital premises.	
LAPPY	8.2.15		Parades as usual. General Fatigues & Routine Work.	
LAPPY	9.2.15		Parades as usual. General Fatigues & Routine Work.	
LAPPY	10.2.15		Parades as usual. General Fatigues. All available men paraded at 9.0 am + proceeded on a Route March, distance 10 miles. Return [illegible] of Unit, on French Leave. Captain [illegible]	

Instructions regarding War Diaries and Intelligence Summaries are contained in F. S. Regs., Part II. and the Staff Manual respectively. Title pages will be prepared in manuscript.

WAR DIARY
or
INTELLIGENCE SUMMARY.
(Erase heading not required.)

Army Form C. 2118.

Place	Date	Hour	Summary of Events and Information	Remarks and references to Appendices
CAPPY	11.2.17	–	Recent convalescent room in the Hospital [illegible] and re-opened the Dental Department which was closed down in June last owing to [illegible]. This unit was then employed in Advanced Dressing & [illegible] Collecting Posts, & [illegible] the Dental Department which had done excellent work in the past was temporarily closed down. A short extract which will give a rough idea of the useful work performed is attached [illegible].	
CAPPY	11.2.17		Parades as usual. General Routine Work + Fatigues. [illegible] for the various [illegible].	
CAPPY	[illegible]		Parades as usual. General Routine Work + Fatigues.	
CAPPY	12.2.17		Parades as usual. General Routine Work + Fatigues. A detachment of 1 [illegible] + 20 other ranks proceeded to ECLUSIER for duty with the 1/2nd [illegible] Field Ambulance at [illegible].	

1577 Wt. W10791/1773 500,000 1/15 D. D. & L. A.D.S.S./Forms/C. 2118.

Army Form C. 2118.

WAR DIARY
or
INTELLIGENCE SUMMARY.
(Erase heading not required.)

Instructions regarding War Diaries and Intelligence Summaries are contained in F. S. Regs., Part II. and the Staff Manual respectively. Title pages will be prepared in manuscript.

Place	Date	Hour	Summary of Events and Information	Remarks and references to Appendices
[illegible]	[illegible]		Parades as usual. Routine Work & Fatigues.	
[illegible]	[illegible]		Parades as usual. Routine Work & Fatigues. Inspection of Gas? Helmets by O.C. Sections.	
[illegible]	[illegible]		Parades as usual. Routine Work & Fatigues. Inspection of Horse [illegible] [illegible] [illegible] by [illegible] [illegible] Divisional Train. [illegible] additional [illegible] Stretcher bearers attached to this unit [illegible] 1st Div Field Ambulance of [illegible]	
[illegible]	[illegible]		Parades as usual. Routine Work & Fatigues.	
[illegible]	[illegible]		Parades as usual. Routine Work & Fatigues. General? Services held for the various denominations.	
[illegible]	[illegible]		Parades as usual. Routine Work & Fatigues. Lieut [illegible] HUTCHINSON having reported his arrival on being attached to the Ambulance?	
[illegible]	[illegible]		Parades as usual. Routine Work & Fatigues. Inspection of Smoke Helmets by O.C. Sections.	

1577 Wt. W10791/1773 500,000 1/15 D. D. & L. A.D.S.S./Forms/C. 2118.

Army Form C. 2118.

WAR DIARY
or
INTELLIGENCE SUMMARY.
(Erase heading not required.)

Instructions regarding War Diaries and Intelligence Summaries are contained in F. S. Regs., Part II. and the Staff Manual respectively. Title pages will be prepared in manuscript.

Place	Date	Hour	Summary of Events and Information	Remarks and references to Appendices
CAPPY	[illegible]		Parades as usual. Routine Work & Fatigues.	
CAPPY	[illegible]		Parades as usual. Routine Work & Fatigues. Collection of Smoke Helmets by R.E. [illegible]	
CAPPY	[illegible]		Parades as usual. Routine Work & Fatigues.	
CAPPY	[illegible]		Parades as usual. Routine Work & Fatigues. A detachment of 1 N.C.O. & 12 men detached for duty with the [illegible] Corps Rest Station until further orders.	
CAPPY	[illegible]		Parades as usual. Routine Work & Fatigues. Church Services held for the various denominations.	
CAPPY	[illegible]		Parades as usual. Routine Work & Fatigues.	
CAPPY	[illegible]		Parades as usual. Routine Work & Fatigues.	
CAPPY	[illegible]		Parades as usual. Routine Work & Fatigues. The detachment with the 1/3rd S. Mid. Field Ambulance returned to Headquarters CAPPY for duty. A further detachment proceeded to CERISY to take over Advanced Posts from 1/3rd South Midland Field Ambulance	

1577 Wt. W10791/1773 500,000 1/15 D. D. & L. A.D.S.S./Forms/C. 2118.

Army Form C. 2118.

Instructions regarding War Diaries and Intelligence Summaries are contained in F. S. Regs., Part II. and the Staff Manual respectively. Title pages will be prepared in manuscript.

WAR DIARY
or
INTELLIGENCE SUMMARY.
(Erase heading not required.)

Place	Date	Hour	Summary of Events and Information	Remarks and references to Appendices
	Mar. 1917		Confidential	

140/2042 Vol 24

48th Div.

1/1st South Midland Field Ambulance

24

War Diary

From 1st March 1917 to 31st March 1917

1577 Wt. W10791/1773 500,000 1/15 D. D. & L. A.D.S.S./Forms/C. 2118.

Instructions regarding War Diaries and Intelligence Summaries are contained in F. S. Regs., Part II. and the Staff Manual respectively. Title pages will be prepared in manuscript.

WAR DIARY
or
INTELLIGENCE SUMMARY.
(Erase heading not required.)

Army Form C. 2118.

Place	Date	Hour	Summary of Events and Information	Remarks and references to Appendices
CAPPY	1.3.17		General Routine Work + Fatigues in connection with the hospital. "B" Section proceeded by Route March to FLAUCOURT to take over Advanced Dressing Station.	
CAPPY	2.3.17		General Routine Work + Fatigues. A detachment of 2 N.C.O's + 22 men returned to duty with the unit, they having been temporarily detached with No 1 Field Ambulance. Inspection of Water Carts	
CAPPY	3.3.17		General Routine Work + Fatigues	
CAPPY	4.3.17		General Routine Work + Fatigues. Divine Service held for the various denominations under Divisional Arrangements	
CAPPY	5.3.17		General Routine Work + Fatigues.	
CAPPY	6.3.17		General Routine Work + Fatigues. Inspection of Smoke Helmets by O's C. Sections.	
CAPPY	7.3.17		General Routine Work + Fatigues. Inspection of Clothing by the Quartermaster	
CAPPY	8.3.17		General Routine Work + Fatigues. Inspection of Water	

1577 Wt. W10791/1773 500,000 1/15 D. D. & L. A.D.S.S./Forms/C. 2118.

Instructions regarding War Diaries and Intelligence Summaries are contained in F. S. Regs., Part II. and the Staff Manual respectively. Title pages will be prepared in manuscript.

WAR DIARY
or
INTELLIGENCE SUMMARY.
(Erase heading not required.)

Army Form C. 2118.

Place	Date	Hour	Summary of Events and Information	Remarks and references to Appendices
L'APPY	8.2.17		Bottles by O.C. Sections.	
L'APPY	9.2.17		General Routine Work & Fatigues	
L'APPY	10.2.17		General Routine Work & Fatigues. The Box Respirators were tested and the necessary exchanges made	
L'APPY	11.2.17		General Routine Work & Fatigues. Divine Service held under Divisional Arrangements	
L'APPY	12.2.17		General Routine Work & Fatigues	
L'APPY	13.2.17		General Routine Work & Fatigues. Lieut D.S.E. MILLIGAN is taken on the strength of the Unit having reported from the Base.	
L'APPY	14.2.17		General Routine Work & Fatigues. Capt. H.F.W. BREDDICKER evacuated to Casualty Clearing Station, sick P.U.O.	
L'APPY	15.2.17		General Routine Work & Fatigues. Inspection of Water Bottles by O.C. Sections.	
L'APPY	16.2.17		General Routine Work & Fatigues. Inspection of Water Carts.	

1577 Wt. W10791/1773 500,000 1/15 D. D. & L. A.D.S.S./Forms/C. 2118.

WAR DIARY
or
INTELLIGENCE SUMMARY.
(Erase heading not required.)

Army Form C. 2118.

Instructions regarding War Diaries and Intelligence Summaries are contained in F. S. Regs., Part II. and the Staff Manual respectively. Title pages will be prepared in manuscript.

Place	Date	Hour	Summary of Events and Information	Remarks and references to Appendices
CAPPY	17.3.17		General Routine Work + Fatigues	
CAPPY	18.3.17		General Routine Work + Fatigues. Divine Service held under Divisional arrangements. Inspection of Water Carts by Commanding Officer.	
CAPPY	19.3.17		General Routine Work + Fatigues.	
CAPPY	20.3.17		General Routine Work + Fatigues. Inspection of Smoke Helmets by O's C. Sections.	
CAPPY	21.3.17		General Routine Work + Fatigues. Inspection of Clothing by the Quartermaster	
CAPPY	22.3.17		General Routine Work + Fatigues. Inspection of Water Bottles by O's C. Sections	
CAPPY	23.3.17		General Routine Work + Fatigues. "B" Section proceeded to PERONNE to open up Dressing Station. One Officer was detached on duty in the Forward Area to administer to the civilian population who were left behind by the enemy	

Instructions regarding War Diaries and Intelligence Summaries are contained in F. S. Regs., Part II. and the Staff Manual respectively. Title pages will be prepared in manuscript.

WAR DIARY
or
INTELLIGENCE SUMMARY.
(Erase heading not required.)

Army Form C. 2118.

Place	Date	Hour	Summary of Events and Information	Remarks and references to Appendices
CAPPY	24.3.17		General Routine Work and Fatigues.	
CAPPY	25.3.17		General Routine Work and Fatigues. Divine Service held under Divisional arrangements. Received orders to proceed forward to PERRONNE on the 26th inst.	
CAPPY	26.3.17		6.0 am Reveille. 6.45 am. Parade for fatigues. 7.30 am. Breakfast. 9.45 am. Parade Full Marching Order, proceeded by Cross Roads to PERRONNE, arriving at destination at 2 pm. Took over the premises of the Civil Hospital, Rue de Beranger PERRONNE, & formed a main dressing station. Sick and wounded collected from area East of River Somme.	
PERRONNE	27.3.17		A good deal of fatigue work was necessary owing to the buildings being considerably damaged not only by shell fire, but caused by the enemy before vacating the town. The necessary fatigues were carried out. Doors and windows built in.	

1577 Wt. W10791/1773 500,000 1/15 D. D. & L. A.D.S.S./Forms/C. 2118.

Instructions regarding War Diaries and Intelligence Summaries are contained in F. S. Regs., Part II. and the Staff Manual respectively. Title pages will be prepared in manuscript.

WAR DIARY
or
INTELLIGENCE SUMMARY.
(Erase heading not required.)

Army Form C. 2118.

Place	Date	Hour	Summary of Events and Information	Remarks and references to Appendices
PERRONNE	27.3.17		And General repairs were carried out as far as possible.	
PERRONNE	28.3.17		General Routine Work + Fatigues. "A" Section under Major [illegible] were responsible for the Medical Work of the Dressing Station, the remainder of the personnel were employed on fatigues in renovating the premises	
PERRONNE	29.3.17		Routine Work and fatigues performed.	
PERRONNE	30.3.17		Routine Work and fatigues performed.	
PERRONNE	31.3.17		Routine Work and fatigues performed.	
			General Remarks.	
			During the period the Unit was stationed at CAPPY, it was suggested that evacuation of patients to Casualty Clearing Stations, might be carried out by means of barges of the Inland Water Transport Services. The Canal	

Instructions regarding War Diaries and Intelligence Summaries are contained in F. S. Regs., Part II. and the Staff Manual respectively. Title pages will be prepared in manuscript.

WAR DIARY
or
INTELLIGENCE SUMMARY.
(Erase heading not required.)

Army Form C. 2118.

Place	Date	Hour	Summary of Events and Information	Remarks and references to Appendices
			ran at the rear of the hospital buildings, and the necessary arrangements were made to convert the buildings nearest the canal as Evacuation Wards. A covered passage was erected from the entrance of the Evacuation Ward to the canal, so that in case of wet weather, patients would be kept as dry as possible & so save them considerable inconvenience. This system of evacuation had not been put into practice when this Unit moved forward to PERRONNE.	
			Dental Dept.	
			This department did a considerable amount of work up to the time the Unit left [illegible]. It has not yet re-opened.	

[signature]
LIEUT. COL. R.A.M.C.T.
COMMANDING, 1st 3.M.F. AMBULANCE.

April. 1917.

48th Div

140/20-6

1/1st South Midland F.A.

Instructions regarding War Diaries and Intelligence Summaries are contained in F. S. Regs., Part II. and the Staff Manual respectively. Title pages will be prepared in manuscript.

WAR DIARY
or
INTELLIGENCE SUMMARY.
(*Erase heading not required.*)

Army Form C. 2118.

Vol 25

Place	Date	Hour	Summary of Events and Information	Remarks and references to Appendices
			1/1st South Midland Field Ambulance	
			War Diary	
			From 1st April 1915 to 30th April 1915	

1577 Wt. W10791/1773 500,000 1/15 D. D. & L. A.D.S.S./Forms/C. 2118.

Instructions regarding War Diaries and Intelligence Summaries are contained in F. S. Regs., Part II. and the Staff Manual respectively. Title pages will be prepared in manuscript.

WAR DIARY
or
INTELLIGENCE SUMMARY.
(Erase heading not required.)

Army Form C. 2118.

Place	Date	Hour	Summary of Events and Information	Remarks and references to Appendices
PERRONNE	1.4.17		6.0 am Reveille. 7.30 am. Breakfast. 9.0 am Parade. Inspection by Commanding Officer. 9.0 p.m. Roll Call. 9.20 p.m. Lights Out. Hospital Staff paraded at 7 am & were relieved by Hospital Night Staff at 7 p.m. The Hospital Day Staff were warned to hold themselves in readiness for night duty, as at the present time the Division being in action, and when fighting taking place, Casualties were expected and the necessary arrangements made. Divine Services held for the various denominations under Divisional arrangements. During the morning two Italian Officers paid a visit to the hospital & Dressing Station premises to ascertain the system of treatment, evacuation etc. Number of cases passed through during day Sick 51, Wounded 69, German Wounded Prisoners 9. Lieutenants Nathaniel Lampton Lucas & Leopold Stanley DAVISON having reported their arrival are taken on the strength of the Unit accordingly.	

Instructions regarding War Diaries and Intelligence Summaries are contained in F. S. Regs., Part II. and the Staff Manual respectively. Title pages will be prepared in manuscript.

WAR DIARY
or
INTELLIGENCE SUMMARY.
(Erase heading not required.)

Army Form C. 2118.

Place	Date	Hour	Summary of Events and Information	Remarks and references to Appendices
PERRONNE	1.4.1[illegible]		[illegible].0 am Reveille. [illegible] am. Breakfast. 9.0 am Parade. Inspection by Commanding Officer. 9.0 p.m. Roll Call. 9.30 p.m. Lights Out. Hospital Staff paraded at [illegible] am & were relieved by Hospital Night Staff at [illegible] pm. The Hospital Day Staff were warned to hold themselves in readiness for night duty, as at the present time the Division being in action, and heavy fighting taking place, casualties were expected and the necessary arrangements made. Divine Services held for the various denominations under Divisional arrangements. During the morning two Italian Officers paid a visit to the Hospital & Dressing Station premises to ascertain the system of treatment, evacuation etc. Number of cases passed through during day Sick [illegible] Wounded [illegible] German Wounded Prisoners [illegible]. Lieutenants Nathaniel Sampson [illegible] & Leonard Stanley DAVISON, having reported their arrival were taken on the strength of the Unit accordingly.	

1577 Wt. W10791/1773 500,000 1/15 D. D. & L. A.D.S.S./Forms/C. 2118.

Instructions regarding War Diaries and Intelligence Summaries are contained in F. S. Regs., Part II. and the Staff Manual respectively. Title pages will be prepared in manuscript.

WAR DIARY
or
INTELLIGENCE SUMMARY.
(Erase heading not required.)

Army Form C. 2118.

Place	Date	Hour	Summary of Events and Information	Remarks and references to Appendices
PERRONNE	2.4.17		Parades as usual for Fatigue parties and Hospital Staff. Renovation of the premises still in progress & being carried out as expeditiously as possible. A.D. of M.S. 48th Division called in the morning and had a tour of inspection round the premises. The following scheme was commenced as from to-day. The hospital will be divided into (a) "A" Block:- Wards 1, 2 & 3 and the smaller wards attached. "B" Block:- Remainder of Wards. (b) Dressing Station:- Reception, Dressing & Operating Rooms & Evacuation Ward. Ward 1 to be kept only for wounded. 2. Wounded disposed of as follows. a. for direct evacuation to Evacuation Ward. b. other cases in Ward 1. Urgent cases evacuated by our own cars or special M.A. Convoy cars at any time. Other cases by Motor Ambulance Convoy at definite time. All cases to be seen by a Medical Officer shortly before evacuation. Medical Officers were accordingly detailed for the various duties. Lionel Sinclair (Surgical	

Instructions regarding War Diaries and Intelligence Summaries are contained in F. S. Regs., Part II. and the Staff Manual respectively. Title pages will be prepared in manuscript.

WAR DIARY
or
INTELLIGENCE SUMMARY.
(Erase heading not required.)

Army Form C. 2118.

Place	Date	Hour	Summary of Events and Information	Remarks and references to Appendices
PERONNE	2.4.17		Parades as usual for Fatigue parties and Hospital Staff. Renovation of the premises still in progress & being carried out as expeditiously as possible. A.D. of M.S. 46th Division called in the morning and had a tour of inspection round the premises. The following scheme was commenced as from to-day. The hospital will be divided into (a) "A" Block:- Wards 1, 2 & 3 and the smaller wards attached. (b) "B" Block:- Remainder of Wards. (c) Dressing Station:- Reception, Dressing & Operating Rooms & Evacuation Ward. Ward 1 to be kept only for wounded. Patients disposed of as follows. – for quick evacuation to Evacuation Ward. All other cases in Ward 1. Urgent cases evacuated by our own car or special Motor Ambulance Convoy car at any time. Other cases by Motor Ambulance Convoy at ~~any~~ definite times. All cases to be seen by a Medical Officer shortly before evacuation. Medical Officers were accordingly detailed for the various duties. [illegible]	

Army Form C. 2118.

WAR DIARY
or
INTELLIGENCE SUMMARY.
(*Erase heading not required.*)

Instructions regarding War Diaries and Intelligence Summaries are contained in F. S. Regs., Part II. and the Staff Manual respectively. Title pages will be prepared in manuscript.

Place	Date	Hour	Summary of Events and Information	Remarks and references to Appendices
PERRONNE	2.4.17		Adviser to the Fourth Army visited the Hospital + Dressing Station in the afternoon. An officer also escorted him round Perronne to show him the destruction caused by the enemy. 50 Sick + 10 Wounded passed through.	
PERRONNE	3.4.17		Parades as usual. Fatigue parties still at work renovating the premises.	
PERRONNE	4.4.17		Parades as usual. Fatigue parties still at work (arranged by the [illegible]). The following were the Medical Arrangements for evacuation of Sick + Wounded from present line:- R.A.D.C. posts established at EPEHY 2 Bearer Squads + 2 Wheeled Stretchers. STE. EMILIE, 2 Bearer Squads + 2 Wheeled Stretchers. STE EMILIE 2 Bearer Squads + 2 Wheeled Stretchers. Advanced Dressing Station situated at VILLERS FAUCON, TEMPLEUX LA FOSSE + TINCOURT. Casualties from the line EPEHY – STE EMILIE and eastward were evacuated by wheeled stretchers as far as the R.A.D.C. post at STE. EMILIE thence by Ambulance Wagons to A.D. Station VILLERS FAUCON.	

1577 Wt. W10791/1773 500,000 1/15 D. D. & L. A.D.S.S./Forms/C. 2118.

Instructions regarding War Diaries and Intelligence Summaries are contained in F. S. Regs., Part II. and the Staff Manual respectively. Title pages will be prepared in manuscript.

WAR DIARY
or
INTELLIGENCE SUMMARY.
(Erase heading not required.)

Army Form C. 2118.

Place	Date	Hour	Summary of Events and Information	Remarks and references to Appendices
PERRONNE	2.4.17		Traveled to the Fourth Army visited the Hospital + Dressing Station in the afternoon. The officer also visited him round Peronne to show him the destruction caused by the enemy. 26 Sick + 10 Wounded passed through.	
PERRONNE	3.4.17		Parades as usual. Fatigue parties still at work renovating the buildings.	
PERRONNE	4.4.17		Parades as usual. Fatigue parties still at work. The following were the Medical Arrangements (issued by the [illegible]) for evacuation of Sick + Wounded from forward line:- [illegible] posts established at EPEHY. 2 Bearer Squads + 2 Wheeled Stretchers. STE. EMILIE, 2 Bearer Squads + 2 Wheeled Stretchers. STE. EMILIE 2 Bearer Squads + 2 Wheeled Stretchers. Advanced Dressing Stations situated at VILLERS FAUCON, TEMPLEUX LA FOSSE + TINCOURT. Casualties from the line EPEHY – STE. EMILIE and eastwards were evacuated by wheeled stretchers as far as the R.A.P. post at STE. EMILIE thence by Ambulance Wagons to A.D. Station VILLERS FAUCON.	

1577 Wt. W10791/1773 500,000 1/15 D. D. & L. A.D.S.S./Forms/C. 2118.

Instructions regarding War Diaries and Intelligence Summaries are contained in F. S. Regs., Part II. and the Staff Manual respectively. Title pages will be prepared in manuscript.

WAR DIARY
or
INTELLIGENCE SUMMARY.
(Erase heading not required.)

Army Form C. 2118.

Place	Date	Hour	Summary of Events and Information	Remarks and references to Appendices
PERRONNE	4.4.17		Casualties from SAULCOURT, LONGAVESNES and area between these were evacuated by Ambulance Wagon to Advanced Dressing Station at TEMPLEUX LA FOSSE. Casualties South of the LONGAVESNES - VILLERS FAUCON Road were evacuated by ambulance wagon to TINCOURT. Two Motor Ambulances were kept at TEMPLEUX LA FOSSE, two at LONGAVESNES and two at VILLERS ~~[illegible]~~ FAUCON. These were worked on the "Block" System. One motor ambulance kept at SAULCOURT + one at TINCOURT. The 1/3rd S.M. Fd Ambulance were in charge of the Advanced Dressing Station assisted by detachments from the 1/2nd South Midland Field Ambulance. The following message was received from the Commander-in-Chief "Congratulate the 48th Division on the success of their operations". The G.O.C. of the 48th Division adds his Congratulations ~~& His [illegible]~~ to all ranks of all Units of the Division	
PERRONNE	5.4.17		Parades as usual. Inspection of Box Helmets by the Qualified	

1577 Wt. W10791/1773 500,000 1/15 D. D. & L. A.D.S.S./Forms/C. 2118.

Instructions regarding War Diaries and Intelligence Summaries are contained in F. S. Regs., Part II. and the Staff Manual respectively. Title pages will be prepared in manuscript.

WAR DIARY
or
INTELLIGENCE SUMMARY.
(Erase heading not required.)

Army Form C. 2118.

Place	Date	Hour	Summary of Events and Information	Remarks and references to Appendices
PERRONNE	4.4.17		Casualties from SAULCOURT, LONGAVESNES and area between them were evacuated by Ambulance Wagon to Advanced Dressing Station at TEMPLEUX LA FOSSE. Casualties South of the LONGAVESNES - VILLERS FAUCON Road were evacuated by ambulance wagon to TINCOURT. Two Motor Ambulances were kept at TEMPLEUX LA FOSSE. Two at LONGAVESNES and two at VILLERS ~~[illegible]~~ FAUCON. These were worked on the "Relay" system. One motor ambulance kept at SAULCOURT & one at TINCOURT. The 1/3rd [illegible] Fd Ambulance was in charge of the Advanced Dressing Station assisted by detachments from the [illegible] Highland Field Ambulance. The following message was received from the Commander-in-Chief "Congratulate the 42nd Division on the success of their operations". The G.O.C. of the 42nd Division adds his congratulations # This ~~message~~ to all ranks of all Units of the Division	
PERRONNE	5.4.17		Lessons as usual. Inspection of Gas Helmets by the [illegible]	

1577 Wt. W10791/1773 500,000 1/15 D. D. & L. A.D.S.S./Forms/C. 2118.

Instructions regarding War Diaries and Intelligence Summaries are contained in F. S. Regs., Part II. and the Staff Manual respectively. Title pages will be prepared in manuscript.

WAR DIARY
or
INTELLIGENCE SUMMARY.
(Erase heading not required.)

Army Form C. 2118.

Place	Date	Hour	Summary of Events and Information	Remarks and references to Appendices
PERONNE	5.4.17		Gas Officer, assisted by the Qualified Gas N.C.O's. Lieut Milligan reported to 1/7th Worcester Regiment for temporary duty. An attack was expected during the night, preparations were made for the reception of casualties. "C" Section Bearer Sub Div. were held in readiness to proceed to the Forward Area if necessary.	
PERONNE	6.4.17		Parades as usual. The casualties from the attack were less than anticipated, the evacuation of casualties were carried out successfully. Lieut Davison proceeded for temporary duty with 2nd Casualty Clearing Station	
PERONNE	7.4.17		Parades as usual. Inspection of Box Helmets by Gas Officer.	
PERONNE	8.4.17		Parades as usual. Divine Services held for the various denominations. A detachment of 2 officers, 4 Nursing Sisters & 5 other ranks reported their arrival	

1577 Wt. W10791/1773 500,000 1/15 D. D. & L. A.D.S.S./Forms/C. 2118.

Instructions regarding War Diaries and Intelligence Summaries are contained in F. S. Regs., Part II. and the Staff Manual respectively. Title pages will be prepared in manuscript.

WAR DIARY
or
INTELLIGENCE SUMMARY.
(Erase heading not required.)

Army Form C. 2118.

Place	Date	Hour	Summary of Events and Information	Remarks and references to Appendices
PERONNE	5.4.17		Gas Officer, assisted by the Qualified Gas N.C.O. [illegible] Lieut Milligan reported to 1/6th Worcester Regiment for temporary duty. An attack was expected during the night. Preparations were made for the reception of casualties. 'A' Section Bearer Sub. Div. were kept in readiness to proceed to the forward areas if necessary.	
PERONNE	6.4.17		Parades as usual. The casualties from the attack were less than anticipated. The evacuations of casualties were carried out successfully. Lieut Davison proceeded for temporary duty with 2nd Casualty Clearing Station	
PERONNE	7.4.17		Parades as usual. Inspection of Box Helmets by Gas Officer.	
PERONNE	8.4.17		Parades as usual. Divine Services held for the various denominations. A detachment of 1 Officer, [illegible] Nursing Sisters & 5 other ranks reported their arrival	

1577 Wt. W10791/1773 500,000 1/15 D. D. & L. A.D.S.S./Forms/C. 2118.

Instructions regarding War Diaries and Intelligence Summaries are contained in F. S. Regs., Part II. and the Staff Manual respectively. Title pages will be prepared in manuscript.

WAR DIARY
or
INTELLIGENCE SUMMARY.
(Erase heading not required.)

Army Form C. 2118.

Place	Date	Hour	Summary of Events and Information	Remarks and references to Appendices
PERONNE	8.4.17		for duty in charge of the Operating Unit attached to this Unit. All Casualties requiring immediate Operation were sent by Special Motor Ambce if necessary & the operation performed here, Special wards and beds were provided for these Cases.	
PERONNE	9.4.17		Parades as usual. Fatigues still being carried out on the improvement of the premises.	
PERONNE	10.4.17		Parades & Fatigues as usual.	
PERONNE	11.4.17		Parades & Fatigues as usual.	
PERONNE	12.4.17		Parades & Fatigues as usual.	
PERONNE	13.4.17		Parades & Fatigues as usual.	
PERONNE	14.4.17		Parades & Fatigues as usual. Lt Col. C. H. [illegible] proceeded to 61st Division to take up appointment as A.D.M.S. as from 12.4.17. Major William [illegible] assumed Command of this Unit. Capt D. A. [illegible] having reported his arrival for duty is taken on the	

1577 Wt. W10791/1773 500,000 1/15 D. D. & L. A.D.S.S./Forms/C. 2118.

Instructions regarding War Diaries and Intelligence Summaries are contained in F. S. Regs., Part II. and the Staff Manual respectively. Title pages will be prepared in manuscript.

WAR DIARY

or

INTELLIGENCE SUMMARY.

(Erase heading not required.)

Army Form C. 2118.

Place	Date	Hour	Summary of Events and Information	Remarks and references to Appendices
PERONNE	8.4.17		for duty in charge of the Operating Unit attached to this Unit. All Casualties requiring immediate operation were sent by Special Motor Ambulance if necessary & the operation performed here, special wards and beds were provided for these cases.	
PERONNE	9.4.17		Parades as usual. Fatigues still being carried out on the embankment of the [illegible].	
PERONNE	10.4.17		Parades & Fatigues as usual.	
PERONNE	11.4.17		Parades & Fatigues as usual.	
PERONNE	12.4.17		Parades & Fatigues as usual.	
PERONNE	13.4.17		Parades & Fatigues as usual.	
PERONNE	14.4.17		Parades & Fatigues as usual. Lt Col. [illegible] transferred to 61st Division to take up appointment as A.D.M.S. as from 12.4.17. Major [illegible] R.A.M.C. assumed Command of this Unit. Capt [illegible] having reported his arrival for duty is taken on the	

Instructions regarding War Diaries and Intelligence Summaries are contained in F. S. Regs., Part II. and the Staff Manual respectively. Title pages will be prepared in manuscript.

WAR DIARY
or
INTELLIGENCE SUMMARY.
(Erase heading not required.)

Army Form C. 2118.

Place	Date	Hour	Summary of Events and Information	Remarks and references to Appendices
PERONNE	[illegible]	—	Strength of the Unit.	
PERONNE.	15.4.17.	—	Parades and Fatigues as usual. Services held for the various denominations. The erection of two hospital "Nissen" huts was commenced. The court-yard having been cleared of debris, was planted with shrubs and plants.	
PERONNE	16.4.17	—	Parades and Fatigues as usual. A party of 6 men of the 1/2 S.M.F. Ambce. reported for duty and were taken on the ration strength.	
PERONNE	17.4.17.	—	Parades and Fatigues as usual. Good progress is being made with the increased accomadation which necessitated bricklaying, re-roofing, repairs to windows and floors.	
PERONNE.	18.4.17	—	Parades and Fatigues as usual. Capt. Laird was detailed as night M.O. until further orders.	
PERONNE	19.4.17	—	Parades and Fatigues as usual. The Motor Ambulance Convoy cars (except four) which were attached to this unit for duty, were struck off the ration strength having returned to their own unit. The detachment of the 1/2 S.M.F. Ambce. were ~~having~~ struck off the ration strength having returned to their unit.	

Instructions regarding War Diaries and Intelligence Summaries are contained in F. S. Regs., Part II. and the Staff Manual respectively. Title pages will be prepared in manuscript.

WAR DIARY
or
INTELLIGENCE SUMMARY.
(Erase heading not required.)

Army Form C. 2118.

Place	Date	Hour	Summary of Events and Information	Remarks and references to Appendices
PERONNE	14.4.17	—	[illegible]	
PERONNE.	15.4.17	—	Parades and fatigues as usual. Services held for the various denominations. The erection of two hospital "Nissen" huts was commenced. The court yard having been cleared of debris was planted with shrubs and plants.	
PERONNE	16.4.17	—	Parades and fatigues as usual. A party of 6 men of the 1/2 S.M.F Ambce. reported for duty and were taken on the ration strength.	
PERONNE	17.4.17	—	Parades and fatigues as usual. Good progress is being made with the increased accomodation which necessitated bricklaying, re-roofing, repairs to windows and floors.	
PERONNE	18.4.17	—	Parades and fatigues as usual. Capt. Laird was detailed as night M.O. until further orders.	
PERONNE	19.4.17	—	Parades and fatigues as usual. The Motor Ambulance Convoy cars (except four) which were attached to this unit for duty, were struck off the ration strength having returned to their own unit. The detachment of the 1/2 S.M.F. Ambce. were ~~having~~ struck off the ration strength having returned to their unit.	

1577 Wt. W10791/1773 500,000 1/15 D. D. & L. A.D.S.S./Forms/C. 2118.

Instructions regarding War Diaries and Intelligence Summaries are contained in F. S. Regs., Part II. and the Staff Manual respectively. Title pages will be prepared in manuscript.

WAR DIARY
or
INTELLIGENCE SUMMARY.
(Erase heading not required.)

Army Form C. 2118.

Place	Date	Hour	Summary of Events and Information	Remarks and references to Appendices
PERONNE	20.4.17	–	Parades and Fatigues as usual.	
PERONNE	21.4.17	–	Parades and Fatigues as usual. The four remaining M.A.C. cars returned to their unit. Capt. J. Ferguson R.A.M.C. T.C. reported his arrival and was taken on the ration strength. Box Respirators were examined by Gas Officer. Water carts inspected by Transport Officer. The Corps Commander visited the hospital.	
PERONNE	22.4.17	–	Parades and Fatigues as usual. Services for various denominations were held. 1 Warrant officer and 2 men of 10th MHOW Ind. Cav. Field Ambce. reported for duty. Capt. J. Ferguson having proceeded to 1/4th OXFORD & BUCKS was struck off strength.	
PERONNE.	23.4.17	–	Parades and Fatigues as usual. Capt. Mitton J.B., R.A.M.C.T.C. reported for duty.	
PERONNE.	24.4.17	–	Parades and Fatigues as usual. Renovations to hospital in progress.	
PERONNE	25.4.17	–	Parades and Fatigues as usual. The civil laundry adjacent to hospital was cleared of débris and prepared for bath-house and wash-house a boiler was obtained and fitted up.	

1577 Wt. W10791/1773 500,000 1/15 D. D. & L. A.D.S.S./Forms/C. 2118.

Instructions regarding War Diaries and Intelligence Summaries are contained in F. S. Regs., Part II. and the Staff Manual respectively. Title pages will be prepared in manuscript.

WAR DIARY
or
INTELLIGENCE SUMMARY.
(Erase heading not required.)

Army Form C. 2118.

Place	Date	Hour	Summary of Events and Information	Remarks and references to Appendices
PERONNE	20.4.17	-	Parades and Fatigues as usual.	
PERONNE	21.4.17	-	Parades and Fatigues as usual. The four remaining M.A.C. cars returned to their unit. Capt. J. Ferguson R.A.M.C. T.C. reported his arrival and was taken on the ration strength. Box Respirators were examined by Gas Officer. Water carts inspected by Transport Officer. The Corps Commander visited the hospital.	
PERONNE	22.4.17	—	Parades and Fatigues as usual. Services for various denominations were held. 1 Warrant Offr and 2 men of 1/4 MHOW Ind. Cav. Field Ambce. reported for duty. Capt. J. Ferguson having proceeded to 1/4th OXFORD & BUCKS was struck off strength.	
PERONNE.	23.4.17	-	Parades and Fatigues as usual. Capt. Hitton J. B., R.A.M.C. T.C. reported for duty.	
PERONNE.	24.4.17	-	Parades and Fatigues as usual. Renovations to hospital in progress.	
PERONNE	25.4.17	—	Parades and Fatigues as usual. The civil laundry adjacent to hospital was cleared of debris and prepared for bath-house and wash-house. a boiler was obtained and fitted up.	

1577 Wt. W10791/1773 500,000 1/15 D. D. & L. A.D.S.S./Forms/C. 2118.

Instructions regarding War Diaries and Intelligence Summaries are contained in F. S. Regs., Part II. and the Staff Manual respectively. Title pages will be prepared in manuscript.

WAR DIARY
or
INTELLIGENCE SUMMARY.
(Erase heading not required.)

Army Form C. 2118.

Place	Date	Hour	Summary of Events and Information	Remarks and references to Appendices
PERONNE	26.4.17	—	Parades and Fatigues as usual. A. Section moved to new billets and the rooms thus vacated were prepared for wards for contact cases. All refuse removed from buildings, court-yard, etc. is being incinerated.	
PERONNE	27.4.17	—	Parades and Fatigues as usual. Rev. E.A. Matheson (U.B) reported for duty. A large ward was specially prepared for gas cases and fitted up with the necessary appliances.	
PERONNE	28.4.17	—	Parades and Fatigues as usual. Lieut. L.S. Dawson reported for duty from C.C.S. The Operating unit (less 2 nursing sisters) returned to their unit.	
PERONNE	29.4.17	—	Parades and Fatigues as usual. The 2 nursing sisters who had been left behind rejoined their unit.	
PERONNE	30.4.17	—	Parades and Fatigues as usual. Capt. W.C. Hodges proceeded to take temporary medical charge of the 1/8 WORCESTERS.	

William W. Lao
Major R.A.M.C.T.
COMMANDING, 1st S.M.F. AMBULANCE.

1577 Wt. W10791/1773 500,000 1/15 D. D. & L. A.D.S.S./Forms/C. 2118.

Army Form C. 2118.

Instructions regarding War Diaries and Intelligence Summaries are contained in F. S. Regs., Part II. and the Staff Manual respectively. Title pages will be prepared in manuscript.

WAR DIARY
or
INTELLIGENCE SUMMARY.
(Erase heading not required.)

Place	Date	Hour	Summary of Events and Information	Remarks and references to Appendices
PERONNE	26.4.17	—	Parades and Fatigues as usual. A. Section moved to new billets and the rooms thus vacated were prepared for wards for contacts cases. All refuse removed from buildings, court-yard, etc, is being incinerated.	
PERONNE	27.4.17	—	Parades and Fatigues as usual. Rev. E. A. Matheson (U.B) reported for duty. A large ward was specially prepared for gas cases and fitted up with the necessary appliances.	
PERONNE	28.4.17	—	Parades and Fatigues as usual. Lieut. L. S. Davison reported for duty from C.C.S. The Operating unit (less 2 nursing sisters) returned to their unit.	
PERONNE	29.4.17	—	Parades and Fatigues as usual. The 2 nursing sisters who had been left behind rejoined their unit.	
PERONNE	30.4.17	—	Parades and Fatigues as usual. Capt. W. C. Hodges proceeded to take temporary medical charge of the 1/8 WOCESTRS.	

[illegible] Major

~~LIEUT. COL.~~ R.A.M.C.T.
COMMANDING, 1st S.M.F. AMBULANCE.

1577 Wt. W10791/1773 500,000 1/15 D. D. & L. A.D.S.S./Forms/C. 2118.

May 1917

48th Div

140/2161

1/1st South Midland F.A.

Army Form C. 2118.

WAR DIARY
or
INTELLIGENCE SUMMARY
(Erase heading not required.)

Instructions regarding War Diaries and Intelligence Summaries are contained in F. S. Regs., Part II. and the Staff Manual respectively. Title Pages will be prepared in manuscript.

Vol 26

Place	Date	Hour	Summary of Events and Information	Remarks and references to Appendices
			1/2nd South Midland Field Ambce.	
			War Diary	
			From 1st Dec 16 to 31st Dec 16	

2449 Wt. W14957/M90 750,000 1/16 J.B.C. & A. Forms/C.2118/12.

Army Form C. 2118.

Instructions regarding War Diaries and Intelligence Summaries are contained in F. S. Regs., Part II. and the Staff Manual respectively. Title Pages will be prepared in manuscript.

WAR DIARY
or
INTELLIGENCE SUMMARY
(Erase heading not required.)

Place	Date	Hour	Summary of Events and Information	Remarks and references to Appendices
PERONNE	15.		The usual parades were held i.e. 6.0 am Reveille 6.30 am Parade 7.20 am Breakfast 9.0 am Parade 1.0 pm Dismissal 2 pm Parade 5 pm Dismissal 9 pm Roll Call 9.30 pm Lights out. The principal [struck out] work carried out was fatigues in endeavouring to make the premises more habitable & also clear out dirt debris from other rooms in order to increase the accomodation. As mentioned in last month's Diary, the premises were utilised prior to the war as a Civil & also Maternity Hospital, and on the arrival of this Unit was very badly damaged, not only by shell fire but by the deliberate intention of the enemy on the evacuation of the town. Consequently a great deal of fatigue work was necessary in order to make the premises as comfortable as possible as a Hospital. Shell holes in the walls were filled up, roofing done where possible, windows & doors etc put in as far as possible. The average number of patients passing through the Hospital during a day was 40, this figure includes wounded. The principal diseases treated at this time were P.U.O. & I.C.T. (Pyrexia Unknown Origin & Inflammation of Connective Tissue). The Division at this time were being relieved by the 42nd Division, the average number of wounded being 20 per day, until the complete relief was carried out.	

Instructions regarding War Diaries and Intelligence Summaries are contained in F. S. Regs., Part II. and the Staff Manual respectively. Title Pages will be prepared in manuscript.

WAR DIARY
or
INTELLIGENCE SUMMARY
(Erase heading not required.)

Army Form C. 2118.

Place	Date	Hour	Summary of Events and Information	Remarks and references to Appendices
PERONNE	2.5.17		Usual Parades. Fatigues in Ord. Magazines. Inspection of the 'Box Respirators' to ensure that they were in working order & that the personnel were acquainted with the method of adjusting them.	
PERONNE	3.5.17		Usual Parades & Fatigues. One N.C.O. & 2 men of the 253 Electrical & Mechanical Coy R.E. reported for duty, in order to install electric lighting plant.	
PERONNE	4.5.17		Parades & Fatigues as usual.	
PERONNE	5.5.17		Parades & Fatigues as usual.	
PERONNE	6.5.17		Parades & Fatigues as usual. Divine Services held for the various denominations.	
PERONNE	7.5.17		Parades & Fatigues as usual. Fatigue went in Ord. Magazines.	
PERONNE	8.5.17		Parades & Fatigues as usual.	
PERONNE	9.5.17		Parades & Fatigues as usual.	
PERONNE	10.5.17		Parades & Fatigues as usual. The necessity for further inoculation was impressed on all ranks, & steps taken to ensure that all N.C.O.s & men were adequately protected. The following men (reinforcements) reported [illegible] for duty 425211 Pte C. A. Allen, 425197 Pte H. Bullock and 425092 Pte H. Edwards.	

2449 Wt. W14957/M90 750,000 1/16 J.B.C. & A. Forms/C.2118/12.

Instructions regarding War Diaries and Intelligence Summaries are contained in F. S. Regs., Part II. and the Staff Manual respectively. Title Pages will be prepared in manuscript.

WAR DIARY
or
INTELLIGENCE SUMMARY
(Erase heading not required.)

Army Form C. 2118.

Place	Date	Hour	Summary of Events and Information	Remarks and references to Appendices
PERONNE	11.5.17		Usual parades + fatigues	
PERONNE	12.5.17		Usual parades + fatigues. The Electric light and plant in full working order. One man of the 253 E. & M. Coy R.E. being left behind to run the plant. For the last week no wounded were treated. The Division being out of the line. The average number of sick cases admitted being 40, the majority of these being able to return to their units for duty in a few days. The average number of cases evacuated to Casualty Clearing Station was 10 per day. Principal diseases P.U.O. + [illegible]	
PERONNE	13.5.17		The Unit proceeded by [illegible] route with [illegible] Infantry Brigade to COMBLES [illegible]. See Appendix 1 for details of orders. Personnel in bivouac.	
COMBLES	14.5.17		Unit proceeded by [illegible] route to [illegible] and relieved the 23rd Field Ambulance 11th Division. See Appendix "2" for details + [illegible] of orders. [illegible] Main Dressing Station attached and details regarding the method of evacuation of casualties. Relief completed by [illegible]	

2449 Wt. W14957/M90 750,000 1/16 J.B.C. & A. Forms/C.2118/12.

Army Form C. 2118.

Instructions regarding War Diaries and Intelligence Summaries are contained in F. S. Regs., Part II. and the Staff Manual respectively. Title Pages will be prepared in manuscript.

WAR DIARY
or
INTELLIGENCE SUMMARY
(Erase heading not required.)

Place	Date	Hour	Summary of Events and Information	Remarks and references to Appendices
[illegible]	[illegible]		Routine work. Collection & Evacuation of Casualties according to scheme arranged. Very few casualties [illegible] in the [illegible] were holding the line.	
[illegible]	[illegible]		Routine work. Fatigue Parties engaged in [illegible] Duck Boards for paths & improving the camp accommodation as much as possible. The following parades were held. 6.0 am Reveille. 6.30 am Parade 7.15 am. Breakfast [illegible] Parade for [illegible] [illegible] Parade [illegible] Dismissal [illegible] Parade [illegible] Dismissal [illegible] Parade for [illegible] Sergt Staff.	
[illegible]	[illegible]		General Routine work & fatigue.	
[illegible]	[illegible]		Parades & work as usual. Capt. D. F. DOBSON RAMC [illegible] reported his arrival for duty with this unit from [illegible] Div. R.E. Lieut H. S. LUCAS R.A.M.C. T.C. struck off strength of Unit having [illegible] to 48th Div. R.E. [illegible] this date.	
[illegible]	[illegible]		Parades & work as usual.	

2449 Wt. W14957/M90 750,000 1/16 J.B.C. & A. Forms/C.2118/12.

Army Form C. 2118.

Instructions regarding War Diaries and Intelligence Summaries are contained in F. S. Regs., Part II. and the Staff Manual respectively. Title Pages will be prepared in manuscript.

WAR DIARY
or
INTELLIGENCE SUMMARY
(Erase heading not required.)

Place	Date	Hour	Summary of Events and Information	Remarks and references to Appendices
PEVENY	20.5.17		Parades + Fatigues. Divine Services held for the various denominations. Personnel had inspection + drill with Box Respirator.	
PEVENY	21.5.17		Parades + Fatigues. Major H. McCALL to be Acting Lieut. Col. whilst Commanding 1/2nd South Mid. Field Ambulance 24/4/17 (Authy Gazette No. 135 of "Appointments & Commissions" dated 12.5.17)	
PEVENY	22.5.17		Parades + Fatigues as usual.	
PEVENY	23.5.17		— do — — do — — do —	
PEVENY	24.5.17		— do — — do — — do —	
PEVENY	25.5.17		— do — — do — — do —	
PEVENY	26.5.17		Parades + Fatigues as usual. Lieut + Qr. HERBERT JOHN FURLER reported for duty with Unit. "B" Section Tent Sub Division reported to No. 2 Casualty Clearing Station for duty.	
PEVENY	27.5.17		Parades + Fatigues. Lieut + Qr. Mr. WILLIAM ALAN STEVENS having proceeded to England is struck off strength of Unit. LIEUT. C. BAYLOR having reported to II Corps for duty is struck off strength of Unit.	

2449 Wt. W14957/M90 750,000 1/16 J.B.C. & A. Forms/C.2118/12.

Army Form C. 2118.

Instructions regarding War Diaries and Intelligence Summaries are contained in F. S. Regs., Part II. and the Staff Manual respectively. Title Pages will be prepared in manuscript.

WAR DIARY
or
INTELLIGENCE SUMMARY

(Erase heading not required.)

Place	Date	Hour	Summary of Events and Information	Remarks and references to Appendices
PEUGNY	1.5.17		Parades & Fatigues as usual.	
PEUGNY	2.5.17		Parades & Fatigues as usual.	
PEUGNY	3.5.17		Parades & Fatigues as usual. Inoculation recommenced. 30% of the personnel were done.	
PEUGNY	[illegible].5.17		Parades & Fatigues as usual. Very few casualties passed through the Dressing Station, the average being about 1 wounded a day. A Plan [illegible] is attached which shows [illegible] occupied by the Unit, also details are attached regarding the evacuation of Casualties.	

[signature]
LIEUT. COL. R.A.M.C.T.
COMMANDING, 1st S.M.F. AMBULANCE.

2449 Wt. W14957/M90 750,000 1/16 J.B.C. & A. Forms/C.2118/12.

Secret

Appendix I

144th Infantry Brigade Order No. [illegible]

Ref. Sheets 57c + 62c 1/40,000. — 12th May 1917

1. The Brigade Group will march tomorrow to COMBLES Area. Starting Point Road Junction LE QUINCONCE I. 20. d. 9.9.

Unit	Time head passes Starting Point	Remarks
4th Gloucester	5. am	(a) Route - GERY - 4.
6th Gloucester	5.12	
7th Worcester	5.24	
8th Worcester	5.36	
Detach. 144th Inf Bde	5.48	(b) A distance of 200 yards will be observed between Units.
144th Machine Gun Coy	5.54	
Bde. HQrs + L.T.M. Battery	6.0	
No 1 Field Ambulance	6.5	
No. 3 Company Train	6.10	(c) Transport will march with Units.
III Corps C.C. Cable Section and No 23 Wireless Section	6.18	

2. Advance Parties on bicycles will meet the Staff Captain at Church, COMBLES at 7.30 am.

3. The Brigade Group will move to an area north of LE TRANSLOY on the morning of the 14th inst + the Brigade will relieve the 20th Infantry Brigade in reserve to 11th Division that evening.

Issued by Signals at 5 pm.

[illegible]
Brigade Major,
144th Infantry Brigade

Appendix 2

Secret.

Ref Sheet 57c 1/40,000

144th Infantry Bde Order No. 18

12th January

1. The Brigade Group will march tomorrow, 13th inst as under. Starting Point Road Junction FREGICOURT T.20.a.28.

Unit	Time Passing Starting Point	Remarks
Bde HQ + 1 Sec. Batty	5.10 am	(a) Route via Sailly - SAILLISEL
8th Worcester	5.12 "	
4th Worcester	5.25 "	(b) Following distances will be maintained. 200 yards between Battns, 500 yds between transport of units and other troops, 100 yards between Companies.
6th Gloucester	5.40 "	
4th Gloucester	6.5 "	
144 Machine Gun Coy	6.10 "	
2 Platoon 5th R. Sussex P.	6.22 "	
III Corps Cable Section	6.24 "	(c) Transport to march with their units
No 3 Coy Train	6.30 "	
No 1 Field Ambce / Section No 2 Fd Ambce	6.35 "	(d) The Brigade will march to 48th Divn "D" Area, i.e. Camps at LE TRANSLOY, BEAULENCOURT & BANCOURT. Destination of Units will be issued later or at Starting Point

2. Advance Parties on bicycles will meet Staff Captain at Starting Point at 8 a.m.

3. The Brigade will take over from 143rd Inf Bde on afternoon of 14th Jan, clearing "D" Area by 2 pm. Details of relief will be issued.

4. All plans, maps, photographs, documents and intelligence, relating to future operations, also all huts, tents, shelters, trench stores & communications will be handed over by 143rd Inf. Bde. on relief.

Issued at 2 pm
by Signals

(Sd) L. G. Gatwell
Major,
Brigade Major
144th Inf. Bde.

Relief of 11th Division by 48th Division

Medical Arrangements.

For the evacuation of sick & wounded the main BAPAUME - CAMBRAI Road is taken as the dividing line between the right & left sector. The right sector will be cleared by the 1/2nd South Mid. Field Ambce whose headqrs. are at LEBUCQUIERE (I.20.a.8.8) & the left sector by the 1/1st South Mid. Fld Ambce whose Headqrs are at BEUGNY

	Right Sector	Left Sector
Regimental Aid Posts	I.29.b.2.2. I.24.b.4.2 I.17.a.6.6 I.12.a.5.8.	I.4.c.5.4. D.26.c.1.4 C.30.a. Central
Field Ambulance Posts	I.28.d.5.8. I.16.c.5.5. I.10.a.1.2	I.3.c.8.6 } Relay I.1.a.5.4 } Posts I.7.b.9.3 I.4.b Central
Advanced Dressing Station	LEBUCQUIERE I.12.c.9.5.	
Main Dressing Station	BEUGNY	BEUGNY
Hospital (for sick only)	N.11.c.	N.11.c.

EVACUATION. All serious & stretcher cases from both sectors & walking wounded from left sector will be evacuated to the Main Dressing Station at BEUGNY where they will be admitted & whence they will be transferred to C.C.S. at BAPAUME, the serious & stretcher cases by M.A.C. Cars & the walking wounded by light railway. Walking wounded ~~by light railway~~ from the right sector will be admitted to LEBUCQUIERE & transferred to C.C.S. at BAPAUME by light railway.

All sick from the whole of the Divisional Area will be sent to the 1/3rd S. Mid Field Ambulance at N.11.c where they will be admitted.

At each Regimental Aid Posts in the right sector there will be 8 O.R. R.A.M.C. & at each Regimental Aid Post in left sector 4 O.R. R.A.M.C.

Regimental Medical Officers will arrange with O.C. Field Ambces of their respective sectors for the collection of the sick of their Units, & will apply to them for any medical assistance or equipment they may require.

(sd). [illegible] Young [illegible]

A.D.M.S. [illegible] Division

June. 1917.

140/2230

1/1st South Mid. F.A.

19

Instructions regarding War Diaries and Intelligence Summaries are contained in F. S. Regs., Part II. and the Staff Manual respectively. Title pages will be prepared in manuscript.

WAR DIARY
or
INTELLIGENCE SUMMARY.
(Erase heading not required.)

Army Form C. 2118.

Vol 27

Place	Date	Hour	Summary of Events and Information	Remarks and references to Appendices
			1/2nd South Midland Field Ambulance. War Diary 1st June 1915 to 30th June 1915	

Instructions regarding War Diaries and Intelligence Summaries are contained in F. S. Regs., Part II. and the Staff Manual respectively. Title pages will be prepared in manuscript.

WAR DIARY
or
~~INTELLIGENCE SUMMARY.~~
(Erase heading not required.)

Army Form C. 2118.

Place	Date	Hour	Summary of Events and Information	Remarks and references to Appendices
BEUGNY	1.6.17		General Routine Work + Fatigues. Collection + Evacuation of Sick + Wounded as per scheme attached to last months Diary. Enlargement of dugouts at Advanced Dressing Station and preparation of new Advanced Dressing Station nearer front line in case of heavy fighting. Wounded admitted during 24 hours. 6. Sick. 8. The re-inoculation of the Unit still being carried out.	
"	2.6.17		Parades as usual. Fatigues + improvements in good progress. CAPTAIN W. BOWATER M.C. + 225129 Pte F. Hobbs proceeded on leave of absence to England.	
"	3.6.17		Parades + Fatigues as usual. Divine Services held for the various denominations. Admitted + transferred 16 Wounded + 11 sick.	
"	4.6.17		Parades + Fatigues as usual. 8 Wounded + 1 sick passed through during the day.	
"	5.6.17		Parades + Fatigues as usual. 3 Wounded + 10 sick.	

1577 Wt. W10791/1773 500,000 1/15 D. D. & L. A.D.S.S./Forms/C. 2118.

Instructions regarding War Diaries and Intelligence Summaries are contained in F. S. Regs., Part II. and the Staff Manual respectively. Title pages will be prepared in manuscript.

WAR DIARY
or
INTELLIGENCE SUMMARY.
(Erase heading not required.)

Army Form C. 2118.

Place	Date	Hour	Summary of Events and Information	Remarks and references to Appendices
BEUGNY	6.6.17		Parades & fatigues as usual. Wounded Nil Sick 14	
"	7.6.17		— do — — do — — do — 425325 Private H. J. EDWARDS taken on strength of Unit, having reported from Base Depot.	
"	8.6.17		Parades & fatigues as usual. (Wounded 5 Sick 12)	
"	9.6.17		— do — — do — — do — Inspection of Box Respirators. 425482. Pte. F. BROWN Invalided to IV Corps Sporting School for Instruction. (Wounded 2 Sick 9)	
"	10.6.17		Parades & fatigues as usual. 425002. Staff Sgt. J. OWEN Invalided on 1 month leave, also 425155 Pte. R. L. TROWDER, 425198. Private P. VEASEY invalided on ten days leave. Divine Services held for the various denominations (Wounded Nil Sick 7).	
"	11.6.17		Parades & fatigues as usual. Capt. T. O. SUMMERHAYES D.S.O. & Captain J. McARTHUR having reported their arrival are taken on the strength of the Unit for duty. Captain D. E. DOBSON is struck off the strength of the Unit having	

1577 Wt. W10791/1773 500,000 1/15 D. D. & L. A.D.S.S./Forms/C. 2118.

Instructions regarding War Diaries and Intelligence Summaries are contained in F. S. Regs., Part II. and the Staff Manual respectively. Title pages will be prepared in manuscript.

WAR DIARY
or
~~INTELLIGENCE~~ SUMMARY.
(Erase heading not required.)

Army Form C. 2118.

Place	Date	Hour	Summary of Events and Information	Remarks and references to Appendices
PENSNY	11.6.17	contd	proceeded to 1/5th Glosters. Regt for Regimental Duty is struck off the strength of this Unit. (7 Sick + 1 Wounded)	
— " —	12.6.17		Parades & Fatigues as usual. The left Relay Post is now at T.12.10.7, this Relay Post being moved on account of a battery taking up a position too near the old relay post, to prevent the evacuation of Casualties being carried out with "moderate" safety. (Wounded 3 Sick 11)	
— " —	13.6.17		Usual Parades & Fatigues. 435512 Pte L.T. WINTERS and 435[illegible] Pte. R. BLACKHAM having reported their arrival for duty from the Base Depot are taken on the strength of the Unit. (Wounded 1. Sick 8)	
— " —	14.6.17		Usual Parades & Fatigues. Inspection of Gas Respirators. (7 Sick + 1 Wounded)	
— " —	15.6.17		Parades & Fatigues as usual. Major J.O. SUMMERHAYES, DSO proceeded for temporary duty with 48th Divisional Ammunition Column. The following men having reported from Base Depot are taken on the strength of the Unit 435500 Pte.	

1577 Wt. W10791/1773 500,000 1/15 D. D. & L. A.D.S.S./Forms/C. 2118.

Instructions regarding War Diaries and Intelligence Summaries are contained in F. S. Regs., Part II. and the Staff Manual respectively. Title pages will be prepared in manuscript.

Army Form C. 2118.

WAR DIARY
or
INTELLIGENCE SUMMARY.
(Erase heading not required.)

Place	Date	Hour	Summary of Events and Information	Remarks and references to Appendices
BEUGNY	5.6.17	Contd	E. PALMER 43441 Pte A. T. BASS – 29452 Pte. D. CUMMINGS (Wounded 1. Sick 7)	
— do —	6.6.17		Parades & Fatigues as usual (Wounded 2. Sick 11)	
— do —	7.6.17		— do — — do — Divine Services held for the various denominations. (Wounded 1. Sick 9)	
— do —	8.6.17		Parades & Fatigues as usual. CAPTAIN W. E. HODGES returned from temporary duty with 1/5 Worcs Regt. (Wounded 1 Sick 5.)	
— do —	9.6.17		Parades & Fatigues as usual. Lieut. [illegible] DAVIES returned from temporary Duty with 1/4 Gloster Regiment. (Wounded. 8. Sick. 5.)	
— do —	10.6.17		Parades & Fatigues as usual. (Wounded 6 Sick 6)	
— do —	11.6.17		— do — — do — — do — Inspection of Box Respirators. (Wounded 2 Sick 12)	
— do —	12.6.17		Parades & Fatigues as usual (Wounded 0 Sick [illegible])	
— do —	13.6.17		— do — — do — (Wounded. 1. Sick [illegible])	

1577 Wt. W10791/1773 500,000 1/15 D. D. & L. A.D.S.S./Forms/C. 2118.

WAR DIARY
or
~~INTELLIGENCE SUMMARY.~~
(Erase heading not required.)

Army Form C. 2118.

Instructions regarding War Diaries and Intelligence Summaries are contained in F. S. Regs., Part II. and the Staff Manual respectively. Title pages will be prepared in manuscript.

Place	Date	Hour	Summary of Events and Information	Remarks and references to Appendices
BEUGNY	24.6.17		Parades & fatigues as usual. Divine Service held for various denominations. (Wounded — Sick 7)	
— " —	25.6.17		Parades & fatigues as usual. Lieut Col. W. McCALL proceeded on one month's leave of absence to England. Captain WILLIAM BOWATER M.C. assumed Command of the Unit. Inspection of Gas Respirators. (Wounded 3 Sick 9)	
— " —	26.6.17		Parades & fatigues as usual. (Wounded 1. Sick 10)	
— " —	27.6.17		— do — — do — — do — (Wounded 3. Sick 8)	
— " —	28.6.17		Parades & fatigues as usual. CAPT J. R. MITTON i/c 1 Tent Sub Division proceeded to 2nd British Casualty Clearing Station for temporary duty. (Wounded 2 Sick 9)	
— " —	29.6.17		Parades & fatigues as usual (Wounded 3. Sick 10).	
— " —	30.6.17		— do — — do — — do — . (Wounded 1 Sick 4).	

1577 Wt. W10791/1773 500,000 1/15 D. D. & L. A.D.S.S./Forms/C. 2118.

Instructions regarding War Diaries and Intelligence Summaries are contained in F. S. Regs., Part II. and the Staff Manual respectively. Title pages will be prepared in manuscript.

WAR DIARY

or

~~INTELLIGENCE SUMMARY.~~

(Erase heading not required.)

Army Form C. 2118.

Place	Date	Hour	Summary of Events and Information	Remarks and references to Appendices
Bevany			The collection & evacuation of casualties was carried out as detailed in the scheme mentioned in last month's Diary. Nothing of importance has occurred during the month, the principal work being the construction & strengthening of dug-outs in the Forward Area, and the general improvement of the accommodation at the Dressing Station. Very few casualties passed through the Dressing Station, the infantry holding the line & not assisting in any offensive operation. The number of wounded & sick which passed through the Dressing Station is noted in [illegible]. From the [illegible] to [illegible] [illegible] Dental Plates were repaired by the Dental Surgeon for the 20th & 28th Divisions.	

W. Bowater
Captain
~~LIEUT.-COLONEL~~, R.A.M.C.T.
COMMANDING 1/1st S. MID. FIELD AMB.

1577 Wt. W10791/1773 500,000 1/15 D. D. & L. A.D.S.S./Forms/C. 2118.

9

July. 1917.

140/2364.

Vol 28

War Diary.

1/1st South Midland Field Ambulance.

From 1st July 1915 to 31st July 1915.

Instructions regarding War Diaries and Intelligence Summaries are contained in F. S. Regs., Part II. and the Staff Manual respectively. Title pages will be prepared in manuscript.

WAR DIARY
or
~~INTELLIGENCE SUMMARY.~~
(Erase heading not required.)

Army Form C. 2118.

Place	Date	Hour	Summary of Events and Information	Remarks and references to Appendices
BEUGNY	1.9.17		Parades as usual. Divine Service held for the various denominations. Preparations were being made to be relieved & move into a new Area. Wagons were packed as far as possible. Every vehicle was fitted with four petrol tins full of water, for use in case of emergency. An Inspection was held to ensure that Bayonets & scabbards were complete & in good order, also Iron Rations were inspected. All surplus stores were returned to Ordnance. See Appendix "I" attached hereto.	
BEUGNY	2.9.17		6.0 am Reveille. 6.30 am Parade. 7.30 am Breakfast. 12 noon Unit parade in Full Marching Order & proceeded by March Route to ACHIET LE PETIT, arrived at destination at 4 p.m., bivouacked in field for the night.	
ACHIET LE PETIT	3.9.17		6.30 am Reveille. 7.30 am Breakfast. 9 am Parade "A" & "B" Sections complete with Horse & Motor Transport will be ready to move at 1.15 pm. to accompany	

1577 Wt. W10791/1773 500,000 1/15 D. D. & L. A.D.S.S./Forms/C. 2118.

Instructions regarding War Diaries and Intelligence Summaries are contained in F. S. Regs., Part II. and the Staff Manual respectively. Title pages will be prepared in manuscript.

WAR DIARY
or
~~INTELLIGENCE SUMMARY.~~
(Erase heading not required.)

Army Form C. 2118.

Place	Date	Hour	Summary of Events and Information	Remarks and references to Appendices
ACHIET LE PETIT	3.7.17		portions of 144th Infantry Brigade & will march in rear of 1/4th Worcestershire Regiment. "C" Section will remain and move off with remainder of the 144th Brigade on the 4th inst. "A" & "B" Sections arrived at their destination GUADIEMPRE at 7. p.m. Hospital opened up for the reception of the sick of the Division. See Appendix 2.	
GUADIEMPRE	4.7.17		6.30. am Reveille. 7.20. am Breakfast. 8.30 am Parade for Hospital Staff (day) 9.0. am Parade Inspection by Commanding Officer. General fatigues in preparing the premises for the reception of patients. "C" Section arrived at PANSART & opened up a Reception Room for sick, no sick were kept here but transferred to GAUDIEMPRE for treatment. The Hospital premises at GAUDIEMPRE were very suitable, a rough sketch is attached hereto, which	

Instructions regarding War Diaries and Intelligence Summaries are contained in F. S. Regs., Part II. and the Staff Manual respectively. Title pages will be prepared in manuscript.

WAR DIARY
or
~~INTELLIGENCE SUMMARY.~~
(Erase heading not required.)

Army Form C. 2118.

Place	Date	Hour	Summary of Events and Information	Remarks and references to Appendices
SAULTEMPRE	4.7.17		each can some idea of the hospital premises. The accommodation consisted of large substantially built wooden huts, with waterproof roofs & well ventilated. The surroundings were also very congenial.	
SAULTEMPRE	5.7.17		6.0 am Reveille. 6.30 am Parade. 7.30 am Breakfast. 8.30 am Hospital Day Staff Parade. 9.0 am Parade (except Hospital Staff) Inspection by Commanding Officer. 1.0 pm Dinner. 2 p.m. Parade. 5.0 pm Dismissal. 7.30 pm. Parade for night hospital staff. Inspection of Post Restoration by Section Officer. The Unit at this period being at rest, prior to moving into new area, no special medical work was done. The average number of cases in hospital being 30, the majority of them suffering from minor ailments, who after a rest in hospital were fit for duty again in a few days time. General Fatigues by the General Duty Section	

1577 Wt. W10791/1773 500,000 1/15 D. D. & L. A.D.S.S./Forms/C. 2118.

Instructions regarding War Diaries and Intelligence Summaries are contained in F. S. Regs., Part II. and the Staff Manual respectively. Title pages will be prepared in manuscript.

WAR DIARY
or
~~INTELLIGENCE SUMMARY.~~
(Erase heading not required.)

Army Form C. 2118.

Place	Date	Hour	Summary of Events and Information	Remarks and references to Appendices
GAUDIEMPRE	5.7.17		consisted of cleaning & improving the premises as far as possible, also assisting the Civilians on their farms. The Wagons & Limbers were thoroughly overhauled & re-painted	
GAUDIEMPRE	6.7.17		Parades & Fatigues as usual. The Capt. [illegible] attached No 3. Casualty Clearing Station rejoined for duty. Inspection of Iron Rations. A Route March, full Marching Order, distance 12 miles, was carried out, to keep the men as fit as possible.	
GAUDIEMPRE	7.7.17		Parades & Fatigues as usual.	
GAUDIEMPRE	8.7.17		Parades & Fatigues as usual. Divine Service held.	
GAUDIEMPRE	9.7.17		Parades & Fatigues as usual.	
GAUDIEMPRE	10.7.17 to 20.7.17		The principal work done by the Unit during this period is as follows:- Nothing of Medical Importance to be noted. The following is the programme of training which was carried out during the [illegible] period	

Instructions regarding War Diaries and Intelligence Summaries are contained in F. S. Regs., Part II. and the Staff Manual respectively. Title pages will be prepared in manuscript.

WAR DIARY

or

~~INTELLIGENCE SUMMARY.~~

(Erase heading not required.)

Army Form C. 2118.

Place	Date	Hour	Summary of Events and Information	Remarks and references to Appendices
GAUDIEMPRE	10.7.17 to 20.7.17		1. Brigade Tactical Exercises. 2. Route Marches for all available men, in full marching order & fighting order alternately. 3. Demonstration & instruction in care & use of Surgical & Medical equipment. 4. Company & Stretcher Drill. 5. Lectures at 2 p.m. daily on various subjects: personal hygiene, Sanitation, First Aid. 6. F.A. Horse Transport attached attend lecture on First Aid & R.A.M.C. bearers attend lectures on Horse management. 7. F.A. [illegible] instructed in the handling of pack transport, great care & time was taken in the latter, it being recognised that great difficulty would be experienced, in the event of a forward move, in moving wheeled transport along roads which have been destroyed by the enemy. Pack transport was therefore improvised in case it should be necessary to take forward the necessary	

1577 Wt. W10791/1773 500,000 1/15 D. D. & L. A.D.S.S./Forms/C. 2118.

Instructions regarding War Diaries and Intelligence Summaries are contained in F. S. Regs., Part II. and the Staff Manual respectively. Title pages will be prepared in manuscript.

WAR DIARY
or
~~INTELLIGENCE SUMMARY.~~
(Erase heading not required.)

Army Form C. 2118.

Place	Date	Hour	Summary of Events and Information	Remarks and references to Appendices
GAUDIEMPRE	10.7.17 to 20.7.17		Ord. Equipment & Stores.	
GAUDIEMPRE	21.7.17		Preparations made to entrain on the 22nd inst. All patients not fit for duty were transferred to other hospitals or evacuated. Wagons loaded & ready to entrain. General fatigues in cleaning up hospital premises & billets.	
GAUDIEMPRE	22.7.17		Reveille 6 am. Parade 6.30 am. Breakfast 7.30 am. Parade 8.0 am. General fatigues 12 noon. Dinner 1.15 pm. Parade full marching order. Unit proceeded by march route to & entrained at MONDICOURT.	
	23.7.17		Detrained at GODEWAERSVELDE & proceeded by march route to GWENTS FARM situated about 1½ miles NE of POPERINGHE on the POPERINGHE – ELVERDINGHE Road.	
GWENTS FARM.			Camp pitched & remained closed & ready to move off at short notice in accordance	

T2134. Wt. W708–776. 500000. 4/15. Sir J. C. & S.

Instructions regarding War Diaries and Intelligence Summaries are contained in F. S. Regs., Part II. and the Staff Manual respectively. Title pages will be prepared in manuscript.

WAR DIARY

or

~~INTELLIGENCE SUMMARY.~~

(Erase heading not required.)

Army Form C. 2118.

Place	Date	Hour	Summary of Events and Information	Remarks and references to Appendices
GWENTS FARM.	23.7.17		with D.D.M.S. XVIII Corps Operation Order (D.D.M.S. No 100/906/19/17 d. 10.7.17.	
GWENTS FARM.	24.7.17		6.30 a.m. Reveille 7.30 am Breakfast. 9.0 am Parade [illegible] Order. Inspection of Iron Rations & Box Helmets. Inspection of rifles of R.A.M.C. personnel attached.	
			No [illegible] STAFF SGT. MAJOR [illegible] J. [illegible] LOWES, [illegible]/248668 Sgt. W. WAREHAM died of wounds received. No [illegible] Dvr. [illegible] P. SILVEY. Killed [illegible] [illegible]/248683 Dvr W. RICHARDS, [illegible]/248695 Dvr. H. WILLDAY, & 423549 Pte A. THORNEYCROFT. wounded but after being dressed remained at duty. The following casualties in horses also occurred. Killed = H.D (Heavy Draught) 4, L.D. (Light Draught) 5 Riding 2. Wounded Evacuated H.D. 2. L.D. 2. The aforementioned casualties occurred at 8 p.m. [illegible] hostile high explosive shell falling in the Camp.	

T2134. Wt. W708—776. 500000. 4/15. Sir J. C. & S.

Instructions regarding War Diaries and Intelligence Summaries are contained in F. S. Regs., Part II. and the Staff Manual respectively. Title pages will be prepared in manuscript.

WAR DIARY
or
~~INTELLIGENCE~~ SUMMARY.
(Erase heading not required.)

Army Form C. 2118.

Place	Date	Hour	Summary of Events and Information	Remarks and references to Appendices
GWENTS FARM	25.7.17		Awaiting Orders. During this period the time was occupied in Physical Drill, Respirator Drill & a General "Refresher" in First Aid, Lectures etc. CAPT. J. M. MACARTHUR struck off strength of Unit having joined the 2/3rd S. Mid. Fld Ambulance for duty. CAPT. W. A. BOWMAN is taken on the strength & attached to 1/5th Gloster Regt for temporary duty.	
GWENTS FARM	26.7.17		Awaiting orders. Respirator drill etc.	
-do-	27.7.17		Awaiting orders. 1 N.C.O. & 29 other ranks proceeded to 133rd Field Ambulance for duty at Advanced Dressing Station DUHALLOWS POST ( ). 2 officers & 10 other ranks proceeded for duty with No 12 Casualty Clearing Station at MENINGHEM. Lieut Col. W. McCALL returned from one month's leave of absence & reassumed command of the Unit.	
GWENTS FARM	28.7.17		Awaiting orders. General Fatigues & Drill	

Instructions regarding War Diaries and Intelligence Summaries are contained in F. S. Regs., Part II. and the Staff Manual respectively. Title pages will be prepared in manuscript.

WAR DIARY
or
~~INTELLIGENCE~~ SUMMARY.
(Erase heading not required.)

Army Form C. 2118.

Place	Date	Hour	Summary of Events and Information	Remarks and references to Appendices
GWENT FARM	29.7.17		Awaiting Orders. Respirator Drill. Lectures etc. 425225 Pte J. Gill struck off strength of Unit having joined 3rd Labour Group for permanent duty.	
GWENT FARM	30.7.17		Awaiting Orders. 1 N.C.O + 29 men returned from duty with 23rd Field Ambulance.	
GWENT FARM	31.7.17		Awaiting Orders. 2nd Lieut Davison attached to 144th Infantry Brigade returned to Headquarters. General Fatigues. Cleaning Wagons etc.	

[signature]
LIEUT.-COLONEL, R.A.M.C.T.
COMMANDING 1/1st S. MID. FIELD AMB.

T2134. Wt. W708—776. 500000. 4/15. Sir J. C. & S.

COPY. APPENDIX 1.

SECRET.

RELEIEF OF 48th. DIVISION BY 3rd. DIVISION.

R.A.M.C. ORDERS BY COLONEL C. A. YOUNG. C.M.G. A.M.S.
A.D.M.S. 48th. DIVISION.

29th. JUNE. 1917.

---

1. The 48th. Divsion (less Artillery) will be relieved the 3rd. Division commencing on June 30th and ending on July 4th. After relief the Division will concentrate in Brigade Groups in the GOMIECOURT-ACHIET-LE-PETIT-BIHUCOURT Area preparatory to moving by rail to XV111 Corps Area under orders to be issued later.

X X X X X X X X X X X X X X X X X X X X X X X X X X X

4. The 8th. Field Ambulance, 3rd. Division, will take over the Advanced Post of the Left Sector on the night of the 1/2nd prox. and the Main Dressing Station at BEUGNY by Noon on 2nd. prox. On relief the 1/1st. South Midland Field Ambulance will proceed by March Route to ACHIET-LE-PETIT Area, where it will come under the command of and be allotyed billets by the G.O.C. 144th. Infantry Brigade.

X X X X X X X X X X X X X X X X X X X X X X X X X X X

6. The Tent Sub-divisions of the 1/1st. and 1/2nd. S. Midland Field Ambulances now doing duty at Nos. 3 & 29 Casualty Clearing Stations respectively, will be relieved by the Tent Sub-divsisons of Field Ambulances of the 3rd. Division on the morning of the 4th. prox. and on releif will rejoin their units in the ACHIET-Le-PETIT and BIHUCOURT Areas.

7. On the march fair weather tracks will be used as far as possible and the regulation 10 minutes halts will be observed.

8. Field Ambulances will take with them only their Mobilization Stores and equipment. All surplus stores and equipment will be handed over to incoming units, and receipts obtained for them. A list of non- expendable medical stores and equipment handed over will be submitted to this office for transmission to the D.D.M.S. 1V Corps.

9. Completion of reliefs will be reported to this office by wire.

X X X X X X X X X X X X X X X X X X X X X X X X X X X X

(sd). C. A. Young. Colonel.
A.D.M.S. 48th. Division.

COPY. APPENDIX 2.

Reference Maps. Sheet. 57D and 51C.

R.A.M.C. Orders by LIEUT-COLONEL T. A. GREEN R.A.M.C.(T).
a/A.D.M.S. 48th. Division.

2nd. July, 1917.

1. The Two Sections of the 1/1st. South Midland Field Ambulance marching with two battalions of the 144th. Infantry Brigade on the 3rd. instant will proceed to GAUDIEMPRE and take over the Ambulance Site at D.2.c. 2.5., where they will open up for the reception of sick from the Division.
The Section marching with the remainder of the 144th. Infantry Brigade on the 4th. inst will proceed to RANSART.

2. Officers Commanding Field Ambulances will arrange for the collection of sick from the respective Brigades Areas and send them direct to 1/1st. South Midland Field Ambulance. All cases except urgent ones should arrive at 1/1st. South Midland Field Ambulance not later than 12 noon.
Instructions as regards evacuations etc., will be issued to 1/1st. SOUTH MIDLAND FIELD AMBULANCE as soon as available.

3. X X X X X X X X X X X X X X X X X X X X X X X X X X X

(sd). T. A. GREEN.

LIEUT-COLONEL,
a/ A.D.M.S. 48th. Division.

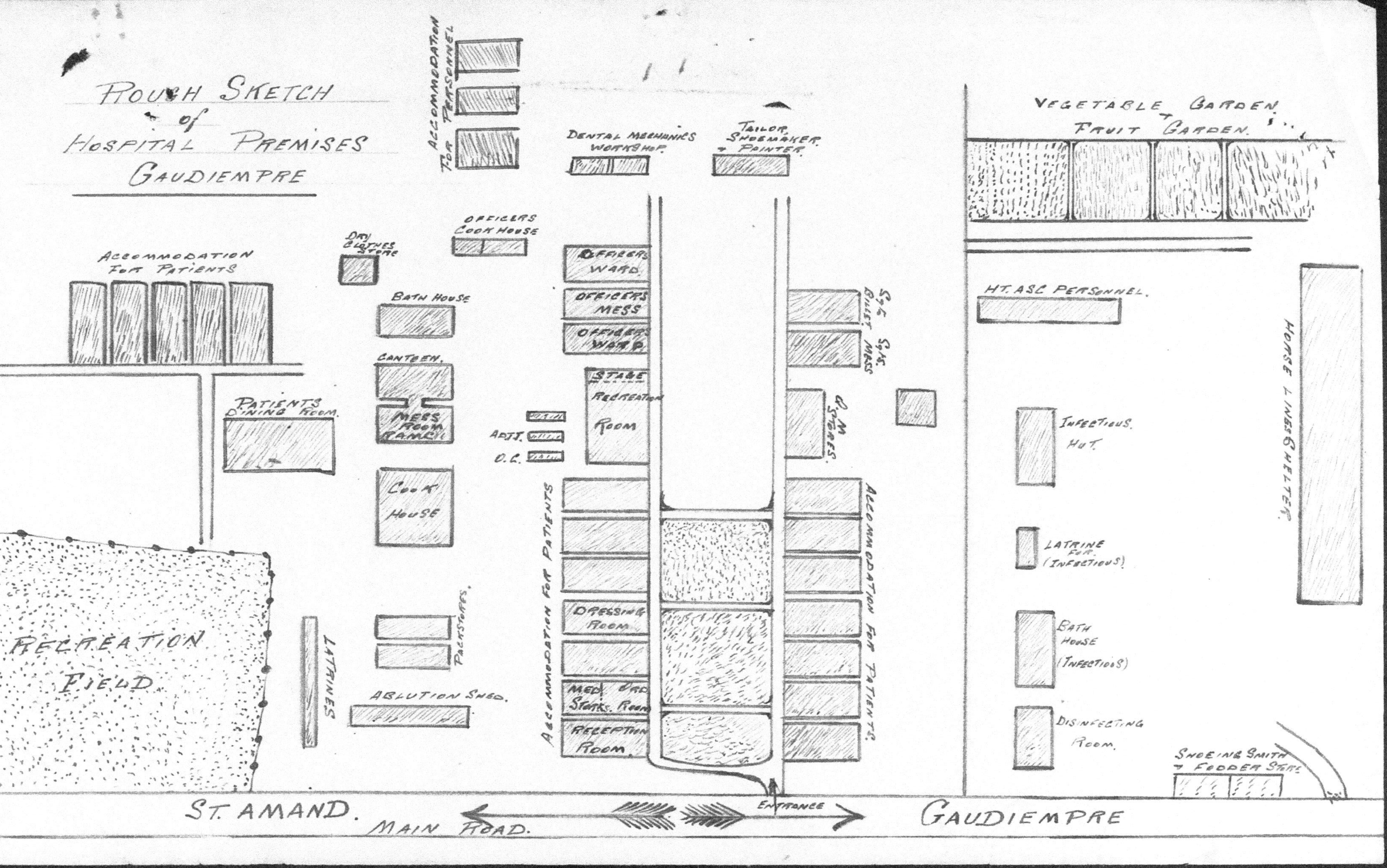

ROUGH SKETCH of HOSPITAL PREMISES GAUDIEMPRE
ACCOMMODATION FOR PERSONNEL
DENTAL MECHANICS WORKSHOP.
TAILOR, SHOEMAKER + PAINTER.
VEGETABLE + FRUIT GARDEN.
ACCOMMODATION FOR PATIENTS
DRY CLOTHES STORE
OFFICERS COOK HOUSE
OFFICERS WARD
OFFICERS MESS
OFFICERS WARD
BATH HOUSE
CANTEEN.
MESS ROOM RAMC
STAGE
RECREATION ROOM
ADJT.
O.C.
Sgts BILLET
Sgts. MESS
Q.M STORES.
HT. ASC PERSONNEL.
HORSE LINES SHELTER.
PATIENTS DINING ROOM.
COOK HOUSE
ACCOMMODATION FOR PATIENTS
DRESSING ROOM
MED. ORD STORES ROOM
RECEPTION ROOM
ACCOMMODATION FOR PATIENTS.
INFECTIOUS HUT.
LATRINE FOR (INFECTIOUS)
BATH HOUSE (INFECTIOUS)
DISINFECTING ROOM.
SHOEING SMITH + FODDER STORE
PACKSTORES.
RECREATION FIELD
LATRINES
ABLUTION SHED.
ST. AMAND.
MAIN ROAD.
ENTRANCE
GAUDIEMPRE

Aug 1917

5

140/2364

1/1st South Midland F. A.

21

Instructions regarding War Diaries and Intelligence Summaries are contained in F. S. Regs., Part II. and the Staff Manual respectively. Title pages will be prepared in manuscript.

WAR DIARY
or
INTELLIGENCE SUMMARY.
(Erase heading not required.)

Army Form C. 2118.

Vol 29

Place	Date	Hour	Summary of Events and Information	Remarks and references to Appendices
			War Diary	
			1st South Midland Field	
			Ambulance	
			1st August 1915 to 2nd August 1915	

T2134. Wt. W708—776. 500000. 4/15. Sir J. C. & S.

Instructions regarding War Diaries and Intelligence Summaries are contained in F. S. Regs., Part II. and the Staff Manual respectively. Title pages will be prepared in manuscript.

WAR DIARY
or
INTELLIGENCE SUMMARY.
(Erase heading not required.)

Army Form C. 2118.

Place	Date	Hour	Summary of Events and Information	Remarks and references to Appendices
SWENT FARM	1.8.15		Awaiting Orders to move forward to relieve the 20th Division as mentioned in last month's Diary. General fatigues such as cleaning wagons, Lectures on "Gas" by the Section Officers. Respirator Drill etc.	
SWENT FARM	2.8.15 to 4.8.15		Awaiting Orders. Captain John Davis [illegible] reported for Duty with the Unit & taken on the strength accordingly (as from 2.8.15) Received order to move forward to Advanced Dressing Station, DUHALLOW (situated a mile & a half North West of Ypres) and relieve the 132nd Field Ambulance, 20th Division by 11 am 5th Aug 1915. Copy of order from A.D.M.S. 48th Division attached which will show the dispositions of the Field Ambulances & also the scheme of evacuation of casualties.	
SWENT FARM	5.8.15		6 am Reveille 6.30 am Parade General Fatigue 7 am Breakfast. 8.30 am Parade Wagons packed ready to move off. 11 am Dinner. 12 noon "A" & "B" Sections Tent Sub Divisions proceeded by [illegible] Route to take over Advanced Dressing	

T2134. Wt. W708–776. 590000. 4/15. Sir J. C. & S.

Instructions regarding War Diaries and Intelligence Summaries are contained in F. S. Regs., Part II. and the Staff Manual respectively. Title pages will be prepared in manuscript.

WAR DIARY
or
~~INTELLIGENCE SUMMARY.~~
(Erase heading not required.)

Army Form C. 2118.

Place	Date	Hour	Summary of Events and Information	Remarks and references to Appendices
	5.8.[illegible]		Station at Dunalloon. [illegible] completed by 4 pm.	
Dunalloon	6.8.[illegible]		"A" Section Tent Sub Division took over Dressing Station from 8 am to 8 pm & "B" Section Tent Sub Division from 8 pm to 8 am. In the event of a rush of casualties both were ready to assist each other. The Dressing Station, Dunalloon as previously mentioned, was situated on the bank of the Yser Canal, one & a half miles North West of Ypres, & was constructed of dug-outs, thirteen in number. These were utilised as 1. Dressing Room, 2. Reserve Dressing Room (in case of heavy fighting) this was used solely for lying cases, 3. Walking Cases Wounded Dressing Room & Evacuation Ward (cases being kept here until a full lorry load had been collected) 4. Kitchen (tea etc. always on hand & given to all cases) 5. Medical & Quartermaster's Stores. The remaining dug-outs were utilised for billets by the Officers	

T2134. Wt. W708–776. 500000. 4/15. Sir J. C. & S.

Instructions regarding War Diaries and Intelligence Summaries are contained in F. S. Regs., Part II. and the Staff Manual respectively. Title pages will be prepared in manuscript.

WAR DIARY
or
~~INTELLIGENCE SUMMARY.~~
(Erase heading not required.)

Army Form C. 2118.

Place	Date	Hour	Summary of Events and Information	Remarks and references to Appendices
Dunallow	6.8.–		N.C.O's & men. The accomodation was rather cramped, two "lying" cases could only be dealt with at a time in each Dressing Room, in case of a rush, especially in an engagement, this meant "Casualties" lying in the open awaiting treatment; then two large shelters were erected, one being solely to keep casualties in awaiting treatment & the other to keep them ~~[illegible]~~ after being dressed & awaiting their removal to different Hospitals by Motor Ambulances. These proved quite useful both from the medical & patients' point of view. The system of working & loading patients was as follows, as each Horse Ambulance or Ford Motor Ambulance arrived at the Advanced Dressing Station from the Divisional Collecting Post, this being situated a mile & half from the A.D.S., all lying cases were taken to the shelter, if the Dressing Rooms were full. — The walking or sitting cases to the Walking Wounded Dressing Room	

T2134. Wt. W708–776. 500000. 4/15. Sir J. C. & S.

Instructions regarding War Diaries and Intelligence Summaries are contained in F. S. Regs., Part II. and the Staff Manual respectively. Title pages will be prepared in manuscript.

WAR DIARY
or
~~INTELLIGENCE SUMMARY.~~
(Erase heading not required.)

Army Form C. 2118.

Place	Date	Hour	Summary of Events and Information	Remarks and references to Appendices
DUHALLOW	6.8.17		as each lying case was dressed, they were taken to the other shelter to await loading on the Motor Ambulances. This prevent a block + the massing up of cases, especially when heavy fighting was taking place + many casualties had to be attended to.	
DUHALLOW	7.8.17 to 20.8.17		It being rather impracticable to mention any particular days work the following will give a general idea of the work done during the period this Unit was in charge i.e. 5.8.17 to 20.8.17. The first rush of casualties came through on the 16th Aug. The infantry commenced to attack at day break on the 16th Aug. The first casualties reached the Dressing Station at 6 am. The total casualties that passed through during the next twenty four hours ending 6 am 17th inst were 700 stretcher or lying cases + 200 sitting cases. The scheme of evacuation as detailed in A.D.M.S. Order.	

T2134. Wt. W708–776. 500000. 4/15. Sir J. C. & S.

Instructions regarding War Diaries and Intelligence Summaries are contained in F. S. Regs., Part II. and the Staff Manual respectively. Title pages will be prepared in manuscript.

WAR DIARY
or
INTELLIGENCE SUMMARY.
(Erase heading not required.)

Army Form C. 2118.

Place	Date	Hour	Summary of Events and Information	Remarks and references to Appendices
			(Copy attached hereto)	
			No 2 A.D.S. was adhered to + worked very successfully. The average number of cases dealt with daily at normal times was forty. The total number of patients passed through the Dressing Station during 5.8.17 to 29.8.17 was 120 officers 2222 o/ranks, 59 Prisoners of War.	
Duhallow	29.8.17		Received orders to hand over Dressing Station to 2/3rd Home Counties Field Ambulance 58th Division. Relief completed by 11 am. Copy of A.D.M.S. orders attached hereto. All personnel of Unit returned to Swent Farm for rest + to await further orders.	
Swent Farm	30.8		Personnel resting. General overhaul of their clothing and equipment + exchanges made where necessary. Owing to the very strenuous time the personnel, especially the bearers had during the last few weeks, only fatigues which	

Instructions regarding War Diaries and Intelligence Summaries are contained in F. S. Regs., Part II. and the Staff Manual respectively. Title pages will be prepared in manuscript.

WAR DIARY
or
~~INTELLIGENCE SUMMARY.~~
(Erase heading not required.)

Army Form C. 2118.

Place	Date	Hour	Summary of Events and Information	Remarks and references to Appendices
	5.8.17		Station at Duhallow. Relief completed by 4 am.	
Duhallow	6.8.17		B Section Tent Sub Division took over Dressing Station from 8 am to 8 pm & A Section Tent Sub Division from 8 pm to 8 am. In the event of a rush of casualties both were ready to assist each other. The Dressing Station, Duhallow as previously mentioned, was situated on the banks of the Yser Canal, one & a half miles North West of Ypres, & was comprised of dug-outs, thirteen in number. These were utilised as:- Dressing Room, Reserve Dressing Room (in case of heavy fighting) these two were solely for Lying Cases; Walking Sick & Wounded Dressing Room & Evacuation Ward (cases being kept here until a full lorry load had been collected) & Kitchen (an orderly was in charge & [illegible] for [illegible] to all cases) & Medical & Quartermaster Stores. The remaining dug-outs were utilised for billets by the Officers	

T2134. Wt. W708—776. 500000. 4/15. Sir J. C. & S.

Instructions regarding War Diaries and Intelligence Summaries are contained in F. S. Regs., Part II. and the Staff Manual respectively. Title pages will be prepared in manuscript.

WAR DIARY
or
~~INTELLIGENCE SUMMARY.~~
(Erase heading not required.)

Army Form C. 2118.

Place	Date	Hour	Summary of Events and Information	Remarks and references to Appendices
[illegible]	6.8.17		N.C.O's & men. The accomodation was rather cramped. two "lying" cases could only be dealt with at a time in each Dressing Room, in case of a rush, especially in inclement weather this meant "Casualties" lying in the open awaiting treatment, then two large shelters were erected one being solely to keep casualties in awaiting treatment & the other to keep them [illegible] after being dressed & awaiting their removal to different Hospitals by Motor Ambulances. These proved quite useful both from the medical & patients point of view. The system of unloading & loading patients was as follows, as each Horse Ambulance or Ford Motor Ambulance arrived at the Advanced Dressing Station from the Divisional Collecting Post, this being situated a mile & half from the A.D.S. all lying cases were taken to the shelter, if the Dressing Rooms were full. & the Walking or Sitting cases to the Walking Wounded Dressing Room.	

Army Form C. 2118.

Instructions regarding War Diaries and Intelligence Summaries are contained in F. S. Regs., Part II. and the Staff Manual respectively. Title pages will be prepared in manuscript.

WAR DIARY
or
INTELLIGENCE SUMMARY.
(Erase heading not required.)

Place	Date	Hour	Summary of Events and Information	Remarks and references to Appendices
DUHALLOW	6.8.17		As each lying case was dressed, they were taken to the other shelter to await loading on the Motor Ambulances. This prevents a halt – the mixing up of cases, especially when heavy fighting was taking place – many casualties had to be attended to.	
DUHALLOW	7.8.17 to 20.8.17		It being rather impracticable to mention any particular days work the following will give a general idea of the work done during the period this unit was in charge i.e. 5.8.17 to 20.8.17. The first rush of casualties came through on the 16th Aug. The infantry commenced to attack at day break on the 16th Aug. The first casualties reached the Dressing Station at 6 a.m. The total casualties that passed through during the next twenty four hours ending 6 am 17th inst were 200 stretcher or lying cases + 200 sitting cases. The scheme of evacuation as detailed in A.D.M.S. orders.	

T2134. Wt. W708–776. 500000. 4/15. Sir J. C. & S.

Instructions regarding War Diaries and Intelligence Summaries are contained in F. S. Regs., Part II. and the Staff Manual respectively. Title pages will be prepared in manuscript.

WAR DIARY
or
~~INTELLIGENCE SUMMARY.~~

(Erase heading not required.)

Army Form C. 2118.

Place	Date	Hour	Summary of Events and Information	Remarks and references to Appendices
			(copy attached hereto).	
			No 2 of 11.8.17 was adhered to + worked very successfully. The average number of cases dealt with daily at normal times was forty. The total number of patients passed through the Dressing Station during 5.8.17 to 29.8.17 was 120 officers 2222 o. ranks, 59 Prisoners of War.	
DUHALLOW	29.8.17		Received orders to hand over Dressing Station ~~[illegible]~~ to 2/3rd Home Counties Field Ambulance 58th Division. Relief completed by 11 am. Copy of F.A. orders attached hereto. HQ Personnel of Unit returned to IWENT FARM for rest + to await further orders.	
Iwent Farm	30.8.17		Personnel resting. General overhaul of their clothing and equipment – exchanges made were necessary. Owing to the very strenuous time the personnel, especially the Bearers, had during the past few weeks, only fatigues were	

T2134. Wt. W708–776. 500000. 4/15. Sir J. C. & S.

Instructions regarding War Diaries and Intelligence Summaries are contained in F. S. Regs., Part II. and the Staff Manual respectively. Title pages will be prepared in manuscript.

WAR DIARY
or
~~INTELLIGENCE SUMMARY.~~
(Erase heading not required.)

Army Form C. 2118.

Place	Date	Hour	Summary of Events and Information	Remarks and references to Appendices
			were absolutely essential were carried out.	
Event Farm	2.8.[illegible]		General fatigues & Guards. Overhauling & collecting equipment. General overhaul of all equipment &c.	
			The following casualties occurred amongst the Bearer Sub Division during the month.	
			435026 Pte J. Edmonds.	
			435204 " [illegible] Parr W — 435229 Pte [illegible] Angel. W	
			435426 " [illegible] Cole W — 435116 " W. H. Goode. W	
			435061 " E. Floyd. W — 435448 " [illegible] W. Lawdell W	
			435125 " W. Connolly. W — 435202 " C. A. Atkins W	
			435506 " [illegible] Watts W — 435126 Cpl W. Hawter. W	
			435529 " Hotmeycroft. W — 435527 Pte [illegible] W. Brown W	
			435217 " W. [illegible] Cox. W — 435245 " C. Allsopp. W	
			435042 " [illegible] Dix. W — 2460 " G. Part. W	
			435107 " R. Turley. W	

William Wall
LIEUT.-COLONEL, R.A.M.C.T.
COMMANDING 1/1ST S. MID. FIELD AMB.

T2134. Wt. W708—776. 500000. 4/15. Sir J. C. & S.

SECRET.

R.A.M.C. 48th. DIVISION OPERATION ORDER No 2.

Ref. Map Sheet 28, 1/40000.

4th. August, 1917.

1. The 48th. Division will relieve the 39th. Division in the line on the night of 5th/6th August 1917.

2. Locations of Medical Posts.)

	1. DIVISIONAL COLLECTING POST.	C.21.c.4.2.
	2. ADV. DRESSING STATION, (DUHALLOW)	C.25.d.3.0.
	3. CORPS WALKING WOUNDED COLLECTIONG POST	H.3.d.5.8.
	4. CORPS MAIN DRESSING STATION	A.23.c.2.9.

3. MOVES. (a) The 1/1st.S.M.F.Amb. will take over GWENT FARM (A.28.a.5.5.) from 133rd. Field Ambulance.
The 1/1st.S.M.F.Amb. will take over A.D.S. at DUHALLOW on August 5th. by 4 p.m. from 133rd. Field Ambulance.
The Bearer Division and Transport will remain at GWENT FARM.

(b) The 1/2nd. S.M.F.Amb. will take over the Divl. Collecting Post and relay Posts from 133rd. Field Ambulance by 4 p.m. on Aug.5th.
One tent sub-division will report for duty at Corps Walking Wounded Collecting Post on Aug.5th. at noon.
The 1/2nd.S.M.F.Amb.Transport will move to field near GWENT FARM on Aug. 5th.

(c) The 1/3rd.S.M.F.Amb. will send the Tent Sub-Division to Corps Main Dressing Station on Aug. 5th. to replace 134th.Field Ambulance.
Time to be arranged by Commanding Officers concerned.
The bearer division will report at A.D.S. on

app 1

August 5th. at 4 p.m. for duty under O.C. 1/2nd.S.M.F.Amb. on line of evacuation.
Advance parties will be detailed to take over stores etc.
Completion of moves to be reported to this office.

4. DUTIES OF OFFICERS COMMANDING FIELD AMBS.

(1) The O.C. 1/1st.S.M.F.Amb. will be in charge of A.D.S.,- Personnel,- 2 tent sub-divisions.

(2) The O.C.1/2nd.S.M.F.Amb. will be in charge of Divisional Collecting Post and the evacuation of sick and wounded from Regimental Aid Posts East of YSER CANAL to the A.D.S.
Personnel,- 1 tent sub-division,
Bearers of 1/2nd.S.M.F.Amb.
Bearers of 1/3rd.S.M.F.Amb.
& Bearers of 1/1st.S.M.F.Amb. when required.

(3) The O.C. 1/3rd.S.M.F.Amb. will be in charge of his tent division working at Corps Main Dressing Station.

5. EVACUATION EAST OF CANAL.

(a) Lying & Sitting cases; By horse ambulance, wagons, Ford cars, wheeled stretchers, or hand carriage to A.D.S. These to be pooled under O.C. 1/2nd.S.M.F.Amb. The evacuation from A.D.S. to Corps M.D.S. is undertaken by the Motor Ambulance Convoy.

(b) Walking Cases;Across tracks to the Walking Wounded Collecting Post.

(c) Special Cases; See A.D.M.S.48th.Divn. No. 3169 d/d 29/7/17.

6. EVACUATION OF SICK WEST OF CANAL.

(a) The O.C. 1/3rd.S.M.F.Amb. will arrange for collection of sick from the Units in DAMBRE CAMP and vicinity at 11a.m. daily.

(b) The O.C. 1/1st.S.M.F.Amb. will arrange for the collection of sick from REIGERSBURG CAMP & vicinity at 11a.m. daily.

7. RETURNS etc.

The O.C. 1/1st.S.M.F.Amb. will send to C.M.D.S. partuculars for A.&.D.book of the following groups :-

(a) those returned to duty.
(b) those sent direct to C.C.S.
(c) those dying in charge of Field Ambulances East of CANAL.

8. RESERVE BEARERS. The A.D.M.S. will have at his disposal extra bearers. These will be detailed as required.

9. WATER POINTS. The following water points have been or are being established :-

Zero	I.2.d.3.8.
Zero + 1	(C.27.a.3.0.
	(C.21.c.5.7.
Zero + 2	C.15.c.10.30.

10. REPORTS OF CASUALTIES, POSITIONS &c. All R.A.M.C. casualties will be notified to this office as soon as possible.
Any alteration in situation of posts will be immediately notified to this office.

11. DIRECTING POSTS. The O.Cs 1/2nd. & 1/1st.S.M.F.Ambs. will be responsible for placing directing posts for the walking wounded to find their way back easily.

12. ACKNOWLEDGE.

R. PICKARD. Colonel,

A.D.M.S. 48th.Division.

SECRET.

R.A.M.C. 48th. DIVISION OPERATION ORDER NO 3.

11th. August 1917.

Ref.Map,Trench Map BELGIUM, 28.N.W.2,
1/10,000.

1. The 48th Division will atack at a day and time to be afterwards communicated.

2. LOCATION OF MEDICAL POSTS.

Regimental Aid Posts, Right, C.17.c.7.0. & after advance move to C.12.c.3.3.

LEFT, C.10.d.6.5. & after advance this R.A.P. will move to C.11.d.0.5.

Relay posts, Right. C.22.c.5.5.
(after the advance) C.17.b.40.20.
(" " ") C.17.c.7.0.

Left, C.16.d.2.3.
C.22.a.1.2.
(after the advance) C.17.a.45.60.

Divisional Collecting Post, C.22.b.7.1.

Bearer Post, C.21.c.4.2.

Advanced Dressing Station, (DUHALLOW) C.25.d.3.0.

Corps Walking Wounded Collecting Post H.3.d.5.8.

Corps Main Dressing Station A.23.c.2.9.

3. DUTIES OF OFFICERS COMMANDING FIELD AMBS :

(1) The O.C. 1/1st.S.Mid.Field Ambulance will be in charge of Advanced Dressing Station, Personnel, 2 Tent Sub-divisions (1/1st)

(2) The O.C. 1/2nd.S.Mid.Field Ambulance will be in charge of Divisional Collecting Post and the evacuation of sick and wounded from Regimental Aid Posts East of YSER CANAL to the Advanced Dressing Station;

Personnel,- 1 Tent Sub-division (1/2nd)
Bearers of 1/1st.S.M.F.A.
Bearers of 1/2nd.S.M.F.A.
Bearers of 1/3rd.S.M.F.A.
5 Platoons Reserve Bearers

(3) The O.C.1/3rd.S.Mid.Field Ambulance will be in charge of his Tent Division workingat Corps Main Dressing Station.

4. DISTRIBUTION OF PERSONNEL. See attached Diagram.

5. EVACUATION EAST OF CANAL.

(a) Lying and Sitting Cases,- If cars can go to the Divisional Collecting Post these cases will be loaded there; if not, then at Relay Post C.22.c.5.3., or at Bearer Post C.21.c.4.2.

(b) Walking wounded,- If lorries are available at or near the Divisional Collecting Post cases will be loaded there; if not, they will proceed to Bearer Post, dressed if necessary, and walk by the duck-board track to A.D.S., being fed at WILSONS FARM en route.

(c) Two Ford Motor Cars will be available from 23rd. Division.

(d) Special cases are to be sent from A.D.S. direct,- See No.3169 d/d 29/7/17,

SECRET.

R.A.M.C. 48th. Division, OPERATION ORDER No 4.

27th. Aug. 1917.

Ref.Maps 1/40000 Sheet 28 & 27,
1/100000 " 5A.

1. New Area. The 48th. Division will be relieved by the 58th. Division on the night 28th/29th inst. and will move to areas as follows :-

48th.Divl. H.Q. at WORMHOUDT,
ROAD CAMP F.25.c. Sheet 27,
TUNNELLING CAMP, F.27.a. do.
SCHOOL CAMP L.3.c. do.
BROWN CAMP A.23.a. Sheet 28,
& A.22.d.

2. D.D.M.S. Operation Order No 10 will be carried out by the Field Ambulances of the 48th. Division.
Receipts and notifications under Paras. 11&16 will be carried out through this office.

3. O.C. 1/1st.S.Mid.Field Ambulance will hand over the Advanced Dressing Station to the 2/2nd. H.C.Field Ambulance by 11 a.m. on the 29th. inst.
He will move his personnel to GWENT FARM where the 1/1st. S.Mid. Field Ambulance will be stationed.

4. O.C. 1/2nd. S.Mid. Field Ambulance will hand over the posts East of the Canal to the 2/1st. H.C.Field Ambulance move to be completed by 11 a.m. on 29th. inst.
In the event of casualties of the 48th. Division remaining to be collected he will leave as many bearers and Officers behind as are necessary to collect them, reporting numbers of bearers and units to this office, and the O.Cs concerned.
He will arrange to leave behind a party of bearers, an equal number from each Field Ambulance, to bring up the 58th. Division to mobilization strength, the number to be notified later.

app 4

He will move the 1/2nd. S.Mid. Field Ambulance to L'EBBE FARM (F.29.d.5.9. Sheet 27) this to be completed by noon on 30th. inst.

5. The O.C. 1/3rd.S.Mid. Field Ambulance will withdraw his Tent Division from Corps Main Dressing Station and move the 1/3rd.S.Mid. Field Ambulance to ST. JAN TER BIEZEN (Sheet 27, L.2.d.7.4.) move to be completed by 6 p.m. on the 29th. inst.

6. Sick etc. of Division : These will be collected by the Field Ambulance at ST.JAN TER BIEZEN at 10 a.m. daily. All the cases which will recover in 48 hours will be detained if possible. Other cases will be sent to Corps Sick Collecting Station.

7. Acknowledge.

R. PICKARD, Colonel,
A.D.M.S., 48th. Divn.

TO H.Q. "A",
D.D.M.S. XV111 Corps.
Os.C. 1/1,1/2,1/3, S.M.F.Ambs.
A.D.M.S. 58th. Divn.
" 51st. "
" 11th. "

A.D.M.S. 48th. Division.

6. RETURNS etc. The O.C. 1/1st.S.Mid.Field Ambulance will send to Corps Main Dressing Station particulars for A & D Book of the following groups,-
(a) those returned to duty.
(b) those sent direct to C.C.S.
(c) those dying in charge of Field Ambulances East of Canal.

7. RESERVE BEARERS One and a half companies of Infantry will report at A.D.S. on Y day at 4 p.m. They will bring rations for Z day and Z+1 days, and will afterwards be rationed by 1/1st.S.M.F.Ambulance. The O.C. 1/2nd.S.M.F.Ambulance will arrange their distribution as per attached diagram. The Reserve Bearers will be provided at the A.D.S. with 1 stretcher per squad of 4 men and an "S.B" armlet per man, before proceeding forward.

8. REPORTS of CASUALTIES POSITIONS etc. All R.A.M.C. casualties will be notified to this Office as soon as possible.
Estimates of R.A.M.C. casualties and other points affecting the Medical Situation must also be reported.
Any alteration in situation of posts will be immediately notified to this office.

9. DIRECTING POSTS. The O.Cs 1/2nd & 1/1st S.Mid. Field Ambulances will be responsible for placing directing posts for walking wounded to find their way back easily.

10. DOCUMENTS OF PRISONERS. The documents of walking wounded German prisoners will be removed from them at the Divisional Collecting Post, stored, and handed over to a representative from 48th. Divl. Hqrs. when asked for.

11. ACKNOWLEDGE.

R.PICKARD, Colonel,
A.D.M.S., 48th. Divn.

To accompany 48th Division R.A.M.C. Operation Order No 3. of 11th August 1917.

SCHEME OF EVACUATION, PERSONNEL etc.

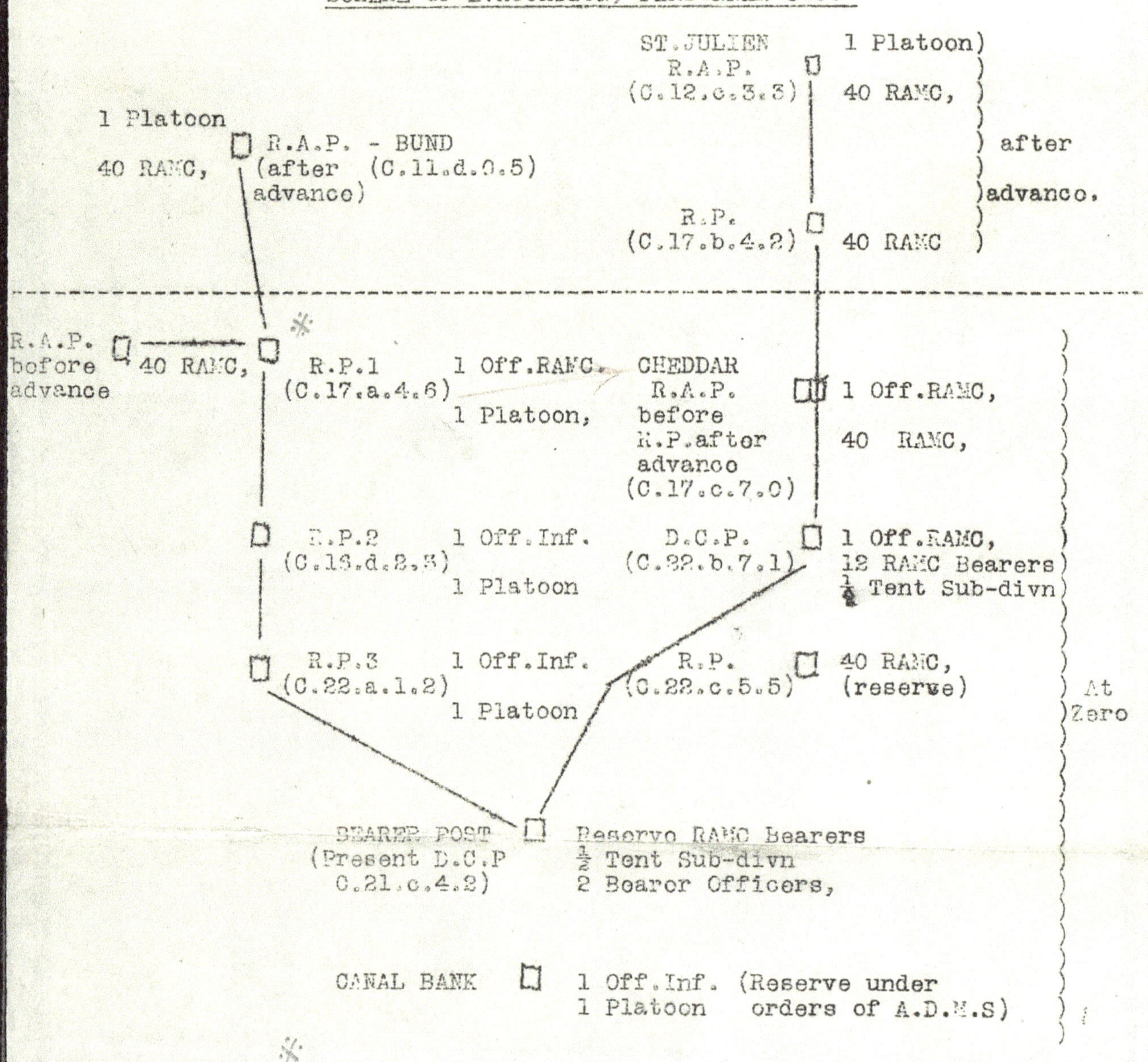

Note,- If cases can be evacuated from R.P.1 to CHEDDAR (see red arrow) 1 Platoon could be moved from R.P.3 to CHEDDAR and the Platoon at R.P.2 divided between it and R.P.3.

Salt 1919

S

1/1st South Midland F.A.

*Instructions regarding War Diaries and Intelligence Summaries are contained in F. S. Regs., Part II. and the Staff Manual respectively. Title pages will be prepared in manuscript.

WAR DIARY
or
INTELLIGENCE SUMMARY.
(*Erase heading not required.*)

Army Form C. 2118.

Vol 30

Place	Date	Hour	Summary of Events and Information	Remarks and references to Appendices
			War Diary	
			1/2nd South Midland Field Ambulance	
			1st September 1917 to 30th September 1917	

D. D. & L., London, E.C.
(A7883) Wt. W803/M1672 350,000 4/17 **Sch. 52a** Forms/C/2118/14

Instructions regarding War Diaries and Intelligence Summaries are contained in F. S. Regs., Part II. and the Staff Manual respectively. Title pages will be prepared in manuscript.

WAR DIARY
or
~~INTELLIGENCE~~ SUMMARY.
(Erase heading not required.)

Army Form C. 2118.

Place	Date	Hour	Summary of Events and Information	Remarks and references to Appendices
GWENT Farm	10.[illegible] to 2.9.[illegible]		The unit at this period was resting – no hospital was opened for the reception of sick. The principal work done was a general overhaul of all equipment & wagons. Deficiencies made up in equipment. Wagons & Limbers overhauled & repainted. Physical Drill & a General refresher course in drill was carried out. Lectures given on the latest type of Gas used by the Enemy. Respirator Drill carried out regularly also inspections of respirators. Super-structures were made for each Water Cart which carried 40 gallons of water in addition, if necessary, to ~~that~~ the water carried in the Water Cart. Each Water Cart when fully loaded would carry 110 Gals of Water. Nothing of military importance occurred & no other operations were carried out by this Unit.	

D. D. & L., London, E.C. (A7883) Wt. W803/M1672 350,000 4/17 Sch. 52a Forms/C/2118/14

Instructions regarding War Diaries and Intelligence Summaries are contained in F. S. Regs., Part II, and the Staff Manual respectively. Title pages will be prepared in manuscript.

WAR DIARY
or
INTELLIGENCE SUMMARY.
(Erase heading not required.)

Army Form C. 2118.

Place	Date	Hour	Summary of Events and Information	Remarks and references to Appendices
GWENT FARM	1.9.17 to 6.9.17		1 Medical Officer 1 W.O. + 8 men were sent for duty with the 58th Division for duty at the Advanced Dressing Station DUHALLOW, reliefs were carried out at regular periods.	
			Captain T.B. MITTON returned from ten days leave of absence on 2nd inst. Major J.C. Summerhayes is taken on the strength of the Unit + is attached to 1/2nd South Midland Field Ambulance for duty as from 1st inst.	
			Lieut + Q.Mr. H.T. FURLER proceeded on ten days leave of absence to England on 4th inst.	
			288255 Cpl. Purdy W having reported his arrival from the Base Depot is taken on the strength as from the 6th inst	
			Major Summerhayes proceeded for temporary duty with XVIII Corps Reinforcement Depot on the 7th inst	

D. D. & L., London, E.C.
(A7883) Wt. W809/M1672 350,000 4/17 Sch. 52a Forms/C/2118/14

Instructions regarding War Diaries and Intelligence Summaries are contained in F. S. Regs., Part II, and the Staff Manual respectively. Title pages will be prepared in manuscript.

WAR DIARY
or
~~INTELLIGENCE~~ SUMMARY.
(*Erase heading not required.*)

Army Form C. 2118.

Place	Date	Hour	Summary of Events and Information	Remarks and references to Appendices
GWENT FARM	1.9.17 to 12.9.17		435075 Pte [illegible] Allen – 435234 Pte J Cox Awarded the Military Medal (Authy 48th Div R.O. 582 6.9.17 XVIII Corps Wire A 85 dated 4.9.17)	
			Captain R.W. MEIKLE struck off strength of Unit & posted to 1/2nd South Midland Field Ambulance for duty on 9th inst.	
			435012 Sgt [illegible] Garland Awarded Bar to Military Medal (Authy XVIII Corps Routine Order No 621) of 12.9.17.	
GWENT FARM	14.9.17		Usual fatigues & drills carried out. Received Movement Order as per 48th Division R.A.M.C. Operation Order No 5 of 14.9.17 attached hereto.	
GWENT FARM	15.9.17		Parades & fatigues as usual. Respirator Drill. All Wagons packed & ready to move.	
GWENT FARM	16.9.17		Parades & fatigues as usual. Transport moved off at 8 am. Billeting Party of 1 Officer & 1 other	

D. D. & L., London, E.C. (A7883) Wt. W809/M1672 350,000 4/17 Sch. 52a Forms/C/2118/14

Instructions regarding War Diaries and Intelligence Summaries are contained in F. S. Regs., Part II. and the Staff Manual respectively. Title pages will be prepared in manuscript.

WAR DIARY
or
INTELLIGENCE SUMMARY.
(Erase heading not required.)

Army Form C. 2118.

Place	Date	Hour	Summary of Events and Information	Remarks and references to Appendices
GWENT FARM	16.9.17		Unit proceeded at 7.30 am to take over billets in new area. Divine Service held at 6.30 pm.	
GWENT FARM	17.9.17.		5.30 am Reveille 6.0 am Breakfast 7.15 am Parade full marching order & proceeded by March Route to ABEELE Station to entrain for new area. (Details of Orders attached hereto 143rd Inf Bde Operation Order No 166 of 15th Sep. 1917.) Unit entrained at 10 am & arrived & detrained at AUDRUICQ at 5.30 pm. And proceeded by March Route to GRAND PAVELLE where the Unit was billeted in barns. A Reception room was opened for the rest of the 143rd Infantry Brigade (48th Division No 189 RAMC Order of 18.9.17 attached hereto) also Copy of Evacuation Scheme)	
GRAND PAVELLE ~~[illegible]~~	18.9.17.		General Routine Work carried out in connection with the Hospital. A system of "training" was carried out. Physical Exercise from 6.30 am to 7.30 am.	

D. D. & L., London, E.C. (A7883) Wt. W803/M1672 350,000 4/17 Sch. 52a Forms/C/2118/14

Instructions regarding War Diaries and Intelligence Summaries are contained in F. S. Regs., Part II, and the Staff Manual respectively. Title pages will be prepared in manuscript.

WAR DIARY
or
~~INTELLIGENCE~~ SUMMARY.
(Erase heading not required.)

Army Form C. 2118.

Place	Date	Hour	Summary of Events and Information	Remarks and references to Appendices
GRAS PAVELLE	18.9.17		Route March in "Fighting Order" from 9 am to 12.30 noon. Lectures given in the afternoon by the Medical Officer on the latest type of "Gas" used by the Enemy.	
GRAS PAVELLE	19.9.17		6.30 am. Physical Drill for one hour. 9.0 am. Parade. Inspection by Commanding Officer. Inspection of Respirators + Respirator Drill. The Tents of each Section were [illegible] for "Airing" + overhauling.	
GRAS PAVELLE	20.9.17		Physical Drill. Route March. Respirator Drill.	
GRAS PAVELLE	21.9.17		6.30 am. Physical Drill. 9.0 am. Inspection of Box Respirators &c by the Divisional Gas Officer. General Fatigues + Routine Work.	
GRAS. PAVELLE	22.9.17		6.30 am. Physical Drill. 9.0 am. Parade. Full Marching Order. Route March. Lecture on March Hygiene.	
GRAS PAVELLE	23.9.17		General Fatigues + Routine Work. Inspection of Respirators. Divine Service held for the various denominations.	

D. D. & L., London, E.C.
(A7883) Wt. W803/M1672 350,000 4/17 Sch. 52a Forms/C/2118/14

Army Form C. 2118.

Instructions regarding War Diaries and Intelligence Summaries are contained in F. S. Regs., Part II. and the Staff Manual respectively. Title pages will be prepared in manuscript.

WAR DIARY
or
INTELLIGENCE SUMMARY.
(Erase heading not required.)

Place	Date	Hour	Summary of Events and Information	Remarks and references to Appendices
GRAS PAVELLE	24.9.17		6.30 am Parade. Physical Drill. 9 am Parade in "Fighting Order" Route March. All available men taken on this Route March. (See S.A.D.C. Operation Order No 90 d/24/9/17 attached hereto)	
GRAS PAVELLE	25.9.17		General routine work + fatigues.	
– " –	26.9.17		– do – – do – – do –. – do –	
– " –	27.9.17		6.30 am Physical Drill 9 am Parade. Inspection by Commanding Officer. Respirator Drill. "B" Section Tent Sub Division proceeded to 3rd Casualty Clearing Station for temporary duty under orders received from A.D.M.S. 48th Division.	
GRAS PAVELLE	28.9.17		Received orders as per copy attached (48th Divn. No 205 26.9.17) All wagons packed + ready to move off. Captain W. Lowater detailed to duty as O.C. Horse Transport proceeding by road on the 29th inst. to XVIII Corps Area.	
GRAS PAVELLE	29.9.17		The Horse Transport proceeded by March Route	

D. D. & L., London, E.C. (A7883) Wt. W803/M1672 350,000 4/17 Sch. 52a Forms/C/2118/14

Instructions regarding War Diaries and Intelligence Summaries are contained in F. S. Regs., Part II, and the Staff Manual respectively. Title pages will be prepared in manuscript.

Army Form C. 2118.

WAR DIARY
or
INTELLIGENCE SUMMARY.
(Erase heading not required.)

Place	Date	Hour	Summary of Events and Information	Remarks and references to Appendices
3 RAS PAVELLE	29.9.17		at 7 am. to WORMHOUDT area. 143 Inf Bde Operation Order 167 received (copy attached) All preparations were made to move in accordance with these orders.	
3 RAS PAVELLE	30.9.17		6.0 am Reveille 6.30 am Parade 7.0 am Breakfast 7.55 am Parade Full Marching Order & proceeded by March Route to AUDRUICQ Station. Entrained at 12 noon & detrained at HOUPOUTRE at 6 pm & proceeded by March Route to L'EBBE FARM where the ~~unit~~ personnel was billeted in tents. Awaiting further orders from Headquarters.	
			<u>Remarks on Month's Work</u>	
			During the past month the unit has not been engaged in any active Military Operations. The principal work being performed was physical exercises	

D. D. & L., London, E.C.
(A7883) Wt. W803/M1672 350,000 4/17 Sch. 52a Forms/C/2118/14

Army Form C. 2118.

Instructions regarding War Diaries and Intelligence Summaries are contained in F. S. Regs., Part II. and the Staff Manual respectively. Title pages will be prepared in manuscript.

WAR DIARY
or
INTELLIGENCE SUMMARY.
(Erase heading not required.)

Place	Date	Hour	Summary of Events and Information	Remarks and references to Appendices
			route marches & general training carried out to ensure the personnel being as fit as possible for any future operations they may be called upon to take part in. R.F.D.C. Order No. 101 dated 25.9.17 attached hereto gives the dispositions & the work of the Field Ambulances during the following month.	
			30/10/17	
			William W. Carr LIEUT.-COLONEL, R.A.M.C.T. COMMANDING 1/1ST S. MID. FIELD AMB.	

D. D. & L., London, E.C.
(A7883) Wt. W803/M1672 350,000 4/17 Sch. 52a Forms/C/2118/14

Secret

48th Division,

R.A.M.C.OPERATION ORDER No 5,

14th Sept. 1917,

Ref.Maps HAZEBROUCK 5A
CALAIS, Sh.13,

1. The 48th Division will move by rail and road march to XIXth Corps Area, RECQUES, on 15th, 16th, & 17th inst.

2. A.D.M.S.Office will open at ZUTKERQUE on 17th inst.

3. MOVES OF FIELD AMBULANCES,-

(a) Transport will move by road,-
1/2nd S.M.Field Ambulance with Transport of 145 Inf. Bde. 15th Sept.
16th Sept. 1/1 S.M.Field Ambulance Transport with Divisional Transport less details;
16th Sept. 1/3rd S.M.Field Ambulance Transport with transport of 144 Inf. Bde.
Times and rendezvous to be notified later.

(b) Personnel: Entraining Station ABEELE, and Detrain -ing Station AUDRUICQ.
13th Sept. 1/2nd S.M.Field Ambulance with personnel of 145 Inf. Bde.
17th Sept. 1/1st and 1/3rd S.M.Field Ambulances with remainder of Division.
Units will march to Entraining Stations and from Detraining Stations by the most direct route; 500 yards will be maintained between Units.
Advance parties will report to Area Commandant RECQUES, on arrival.

4. Detention Hut will be cleared by 1/3rd S.M.Field Ambce on 16th inst. Cases having to be collected after that clearance will be sent to Corps Sick Collecting Station or Casualty Clearing Station. under normal arrangements.

5. Each Field Ambulance will be responsible for
(a) Collection of sick of Brigade group on route,
(b) at Detraining station,
(c) in Brigade Area.

6. Disposal of Sick,- All Sick will for the present be sent to 1/2nd S.M.Field Ambulance at LICQUES.

7. The 1/2nd S.M.Field Ambulance will dispose of sick in accordance with D.M.S.Fifth Army 11/76 d/d 12th inst. last paragraph.
GRENOGE FARM quoted in Memo 44 is about 2000 yds West of VOLKERINCKHOVE.

9. ACKNOWLEDGE.

R. Pickard

Colonel,
A.D.M.S.48th Divn,

Copies to,- H.Q."A"
D.M.S.5th Army,
D.D.M.S. XVIII Corps,
" XIX Corps,
O.Cs 1/1,1/2,1/3,S.M.F.Ambs
War Diary,

1

ADDAENDUNDUM R.A.M.C.OPERATION ORDER No 5,

14th Sept 1917,

8. The Field Ambulances will billet in the following Brigade Areas,-

1/1 S.M.Fd Ambce; 143 Inf.Bde area, NORDAUSQUES.
1/2 S.M.Fd Ambce; 145 Inf.Bde. Area, LICQUES.
1/3 S.M.Fd Ambce, 144 Inf.Bde. Area, NIELLES.

The exact spots have not yet been determined, but will probably be,-

1/1 S.M.Fd Ambce, LOST BARNE.
1/2 S.M.Fd Ambce, LICQUES.
1/3 S.M.Fd Ambce, ~~KMN~~ BLANCPIGNON.

R Pickard

Colonel,
A.D.M.S.48th Divn.

Transport Movement Table - To accompany 48th Div Order No 217 d/d 14-9-17

Serial No.	Date	Unit,	From	To	Route	Remarks,
1.	15th Sept	Transport of 145 Inf. Bde. 2nd Fd Amb. & 1 Co. Div Trn.	18 Corps Area	ZEGGERS CAPPEL	WATOU HOUTKERQUE & WORMHOUDT	Billets from Area Commandant ZEGGERS CAPPEL.
2.	16th Sept	do.	ZEGGERS CAPPEL	RECQUES AREA	BOLLEZEELE MERCKEGHEM WATTEN - thence most direct route.	
3.	16th Sept	Transport of 48th Div. (less details, plus 1st Fd Ambce)	XVIII Corps Area	ZEGGERS CAPPEL.	As for Serial No 1	do.
4.	16th Sept.	Transport of 144th Inf Bde. & 3rd Fd Ambce,	18 Corps Area,	ZEGGERS CAPPEL,	As for Serial No 1.	To follow Serial No 3. Billets from Area Commandant ZEGGERS CAPPEL.
5.	17th Sept.	Serial No 3	ZEGGERS CAPPEL	RECQUES AREA	BOLLEZEELE MERCKEGHEM WATTEN -thence most direct route.	

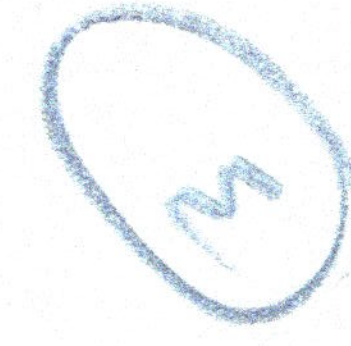

11

SECRET.   Copy No. . . .

143rd Inf. Bde. OPERATION ORDER NO. 166

Ref. maps
1/100,000 HAZEBROUCK 5A
,, CALAIS 13

15th September 1917

1. The Bde. (less portion of transport) will move by rail and march route to the NORDAUSQUES Bde. Area on the 17th inst.

2. Entraining Station . . . ABEELE
Detraining Station . . . AUDRUICK

Instructions for moves of units to and from entraining and detraining stations and entraining orders will be issued later.

3. Units will be accommodated in the NORDAUSQUES Area as under :-

5th Bn. R.War.R.	...	NORDAUSQUES
6th Bn. ,,	...	LOUCHES
7th Bn. ,,	...	LA PANNE
8th Bn. ,,	...	ZOUAFQUES
M.G.Coy.) T.M.Batt.)	...	AUTINGUES
3rd S.M.Fd. Amb.	...	LOSTBARNE or ZURKERQUE.
No. 2 Coy. Train	...	ZOUAFQUES.

Accommodation table and maps are attached (to Bde. Units only).

4. Advanced parties from all units will be prepared to move to-morrow under orders which will be notified later.

5. Rations for the 18th inst. will be delivered at the new area.

6. The portion of the transport not going by train will move under orders of the B.T.O. in accordance with the attached March table.
Time of starting will be 8-30 a.m. on 16th.
200 yds. distance will be maintained between groups of wagons, which will move in groups of not more than ten.

7. Bde. Hdqrs. will move to WOLPHUS Chau. on the 17th inst.

8. ACKNOWLEDGE.

G.W. Dewart
Captain,
B.M. 143rd Inf. Bde.

Issued through Signals
at

Copy No. 1 and 2 retained
3 to 11 Bdc. Units.
12 and 13 48th Division.
14 and 15 War Diary.

March Tablo for Transport issued with O.O.166

DATE	FROM	TO	ROUTE	REMARKS
Sept. 16th	TUNNELLING CAMP	ZEGGERS CAPPEL	WATOU-HOUTKERQUE and WORMHOUDT.	Billets from Area Commandant ZEGGERS CAPPEL
Sept. 17th	ZEGGERS CAPPEL	NORDAUSQUES Area.	BOLLEZEELE - MERCKEGHEM - WATTEN - BAYENGHEM - NORDAUSQUES - Thence most direct route to Unit's Billeting Area.	'B' Convoy to be clear of ZEGGERS CAPPEL by 9 a.m.,

3rd S.M. Fd. Amb and No. 2 Coy. Train will move with Bde. Transport.
The whole will be called 'B' Convoy and will be under the command of the B.T.O..

SECRET.

Copy No. 11

Addendum No. 1 to

143rd Inf. Bde. OPERATION ORDER NO. 166

Ref. map
1/40,000 Sheet 27.

16th September 1917.

1. Units will move to their entraining station according to the attached march table.

Personnel of No.2 Coy. Train to be at ABEELE Sta. by 5-30 a.m.

Personnel of 1/1st Fd. Amb. ,, ,, ,, ,, ,, ,, 9-30 a.m.

Entraining and Detraining Table is also attached.

2. On detraining, Units will move to their destinations by the shortest routes, and will report to Bde. Hdqrs. when move is complete.

3. 6th Bn. R.War.R. will detail 1 Officer and 50 O.R. to act as entraining party for No. 7 train and this party will report to B.T.O. at PROVEN Sta. at 4 a.m.

7th Bn. R.War.R. will detail 1 Officer and 50 O.R. to act as entraining party for No. 8 train and this party will report to B.T.O. at PROVEN Sta. at 8 a.m.

4. 6th Bn. R.War.R. will detail 1 Field Officer to superintend detraining of whole Bde. Group.

5th Bn. R.War.R. will detail 1 Field Officer to superintend the entraining at ABEELE.

5. Lorries will be available to take spare kits etc. to PROVEN Sta. as follows :-

1 lorry per Bn.
1 lorry per T.M.Batt and Bde. Hdqrs.

In addition each Bn. lorry will be required to carry 2 T.M. guns. Detailed instructions will be issued later.

6. A hut will be available in the camp for storing surplus stores etc.
Further details will be issued later.

7. Units will prepare an entraining state which will be handed to Field Officer i/c of entraining who will hand them over to the R.T.O.

8. ACKNOWLEDGE.

C W Scart

Captain,

B.M. 143rd Inf. Bde.

Issued through Signals
at 10 am

Copy No. 1 and 2 retained
3 to 11 Bde. Units.
12 and 13 48th Division.
14 and 15 War Diary.

Entraining and Detraining Table issued with Add. No. 1 to O.O.166

UNIT	NO. OF TRAIN	STATION	TRAIN ARRIVES	TRAIN DEPARTS	REMARKS
Transport and horses of units going by No.5 Train. Entraining party of 6th Bn. R.War.R.	7	PROVEN	4 a.m.	7 a.m.	Field Officer from 6th Bn. R. War.R. in charge of detraining of whole Bde. to go by this train. Entraining party will act as detraining party to train on arrival.
6th and 7th Bns. R.War.R. (less entraining parties) M.G.Coy. T.M.Batt. Personnel of No.2 Coy. Train	5	ABEELE	5-30 a.m.	6-30 a.m.	
Remainder of transport and horses. Contents of lorries. Entraining party from 7th Bn. R.War.R.	8	PROVEN	8 a.m.	11 a.m.	Entraining party will act as detraining party to train on arrival
Bde. Hdqrs. No.2 Sec. Signal Coy. 5th and 8th Bns. R.War.R. 1/1st Fd. Amb. (personnel)	6	ABEELE	9-30 a.m.	10-30 a.m.	Field Officer from 5th Bn. R.War.R. in charge of entraining will go by this train.

No.5 and 6 trains are each composed of 2 coaches (for Officers), 42 3rd Class carriages (each holding 50 men), 2 covered goods Wagons and 2 flat trucks.

No. 7 and 8 ,, ,, ,, ,, ,, 1 coach (for Officers) 30 covered Wagons and 17 flat trucks.

Journey will take about 3 hours.

March Table to Entraining Station (issued with Addendum No.1 to O.O.166)

UNIT	POSITION	STARTING POINT	PASSING S.P. AT	ROUTE	DESTINATION	REMARKS.
7th Bn. R.War.R.	TUNNELLING CAMP.	Road junction at L.2.b.34	2 a.m.	L.2.b.34 - L.2.a.57 S.W. to K.17.b.58 S.E. to ABEELE - to Sta. in L.32.b.	ABEELE Sta.	
6th Bn. ,,	,,	,,	2-15 a.m.	,,	,,	
M.G.Coy.	,,	,,	2-30 a.m.	,,	,,	
T.M.Batt.	,,	,,	2-35 a.m.	,,	,,	
Bde. Hdqrs.	,,	,,	5 a.m.	,,	,,	
8th Bn. R.War.R.	,,	,,	5-5 a.m.	,,	,,	
5th Bn. ,,	,,	,,	5-20 a.m.	,,	,,	
Transport and horses going by No.7 train.	,,	Road junction at F.21.c.97	3 a.m.	POPERINGHE-PROVEN Road.	PROVEN Sta.	
Transport and horses going by No.8 train	,,	,,	7 a.m.	,,	,,	

Distances of 500 yds. between Bns. and 200 yds. between Coys. will be maintained on the march.

No 189

48th Division,

R.A.M.C. ORDER by Lt-Colonel T.A.GREEN, R.A.M.C.T.

A/A.D.M.S. 48th Division,

18th Sept. 1917,

1. O.Cs. 1/1st & 1/3rd S.Mid. Field Ambulances will open Sick Detention Rooms, where they will retain suitable cases of sickness of the 143rd & 144th Inf. Bdes. respectively, for 48 hours, except in the case of Officers, who will be sent direct to 1/2nd S.Mid. Field Ambulance at Chateau LICQUES.
2. They will send all cases which are likely to be well in 14 days to the 1/2nd S.Mid. Field Ambulance. These cases will be sent on a nominal roll and not as Transfers.
3. They will send direct to C.C.S. all cases which it is necessary to evacuate out of the Divisional Area. At the same time they will render a nominal roll of these cases to O.C.1/2nd S.M.Fd Ambulance for inclusion in the A.& D. Book.

4. The O.C. 1/2nd S.Mid. Field Ambulance will keep an official A.& D. Book for the whole Divisional Area, and will render the official Daily State of Sick & Wounded to reach this office by 1 p.m. He will also render all usual returns.

5. O.Cs. 1/1st & 1/3rd S.Mid. Field Ambulances will keep an A & D Book and render a Daily State of Sick & Wounded for the information of the Division. They will not render an A.F. 36.

6. O.Cs. Field Ambulances will arrange for the collection of sick in their brigade areas at 10 a.m. each morning.

7. Field Ambulances will submit separate indents for Medical Stores to Advanced Depot Medical Stores at a place to be notified later.

8. Dental and Ophthalmic Arrangements and list of C.C.Ss are attached.

T.A.Green

Lieut-Colonel,
A/A.D.M.S.48th Division,

3

SECRET

O.C. 1/1 S.M.Fd Ambce,
" 1/2 "
" 1/3 "

Stand fast with reference to para. 4 of attached ORDER.

J.M. Beckton

Captain,
for A.D.M.S. 48th Divn,

24-9-17

SECRET. 48th Division, No 190

R.A.M.C. ORDER by
Lt-Colonel T.A.GREEN,R.A.M.C.TF,
A/A.D.M.S. 48th Division,

24th Sept. 1917,

Copy of 1-7 to Cr...

1. After 4 p.m. today (24th inst.) no cases will be sent to the 1/2nd S.Mid. Field Ambulance at LICQUES by the 1/1st & 1/3rd S.Mid. Field Ambulances.

2. O.Cs 1/1st & 1/3rd S.Mid. Field Ambulances will retain cases which will be fit to rejoin their units within 48 hrs. All others will be evacuated by them direct. They will render a daily state to this office, and all other routine returns.

3. O.C. 1/2nd S.Mid. Field Ambulance will forthwith evacuate all cases which will not be able to rejoin their units within 24 hours. He will collect and dispose of all sick of the 145th Inf. Bde. so long as units of that Brigade remain in this Area, and will continue to render the usual returns.

4. O.Cs all Field Ambulances will be prepared to move under orders of the B.G.C. the Brigade to which they are temporarily attached.

5. In the event of the 1/2nd S.Mid. Field Ambulance not being relieved at the XIX Corps Rest Station at CHATEAU LICQUES before they move with the 145th Inf. Bde. the O.C. will detail a rear party of 1 N.C.O. and 2 men who will be responsible for the safe custody of Corps Stores pending the instructions from D.D.M.S. XIX Corps.

6. O.Cs all Ambulances will hand over area stores to the Area Commandant before they move, and obtain the usual receipts.

7. ACKNOWLEDGE. [initials]

T A Green

Lt-Colonel,
A/A.D.M.S. 48th Division.

(4)

SECRET.

No 191,

48th Division,

R.A.M.C. ORDER by Lt-Colonel T.A.GREEN, RAMC.T,

A/A.D.M.S. 48th Division,

25th Sept. 1917,

1. The Transport of the 1/2nd & 1/3rd S.Mid. Field Ambulances will march together tomorrow (26th inst.) to ESQUELBECQ under the command of Captain SOUTTER. They will rendezvous at the Bridge, NORDAUSQUES at 8 a.m. Route via EPERLECQUES, WATTEN, CLITRES, MERCKEGHEM.

2. On the 27th inst. the transport will proceed to their respective destinations as follows,-
   1/2nd S.Mid.Field Ambulance to XVIII Corps Main Dressing Station.
   The transport of the 1/3rd S.Mid. Field Ambulance to GWENT FARM.

3. The Personnel of 1/2nd S.Mid. Field Ambulance & 1/3rd S.Mid. Field Ambulance will entrain at ARDRUICQ on the 27th inst. at a time to be notified later, and will detrain at BRIELEN.

4. Thence the 1/2nd S.Mid. Field Ambulance will proceed to XVIII Corps Main Dressing Station and relieve the 2/1st Home Counties Field Ambulance at that Station on 27th/28th inst. O.C. 1/2nd S.Mid. Field Ambulance will detail 1 Officer with 1 Tent Sub-division to relieve the Tent Sub-division of the 2/1st Home Counties Field Ambulance at XVIII Corps Walking Wounded Collecting Post on the 28th inst.

5. The 1/3rd S.Mid. Field Ambulance will relieve the 2/2nd & 2/3rd Home Counties Field Ambulances at the Advanced Dressing DUHALLOW Station, Divisional Collecting Post, and Relay Posts on the 28th inst.

6. O.C. 1/2nd S.Mid. Field Ambulance will, on arriving in the new area, arrange with the O.C. No 24 M.A.C. for the collection of the Sick of 48th Division.in the forward area.

7. The 1/1st S.Mid. Field Ambulance will collect the Sick of the Division from the whole ~~area~~ of the back area, and evacuate cases which will not be well in 48 hours, and will continue to render the usual returns to this office.

8. Completion of moves to be reported to this office.

9. ACKNOWLEDGE.

T.A.Green

Lt-Colonel,
A/A.D.M.S. 48th Division

"C" Form.

MESSAGES AND SIGNALS.

Army Form C. 2123.
(In books of 100.)

No. of Message..............

Prefix.......Code.......Words.......	Received.	Sent, or sent out.	Office Stamp.
£ s. d.	From	At.........m.	28.IX.17. TELEGRAPHS
Charges to Collect	By ...R.F.....	To	
Service Instructions.		By..........	

Handed in at....YDE.....Office...7.5...m. Received....7.5.....m.

TO 1st 2nd Bat.

*Sender's Number	Day of Month	In reply to Number	AAA
G 819	28		

Ref	5/305	Para	1
starting	point	should	read
Road	junction	400	Yds
N.W	of	MONNE	COVE

FROM 48 Div.

TIME & PLACE

*This line should be erased if not required

C. & R. 7330 Wt. W14832/M/1523 100,000. 2/17. (E930). Forms C/2123.

Copy No...6....

48th Division
S/305. 26/9/1917.

SECRET.

ORDERS for move of Division in connection with Addendum No. 1 to 48th Division Order No. 218.

Order of March.
143 Bde Train Waggons
144 " "
No. 2 Coy Div. Train.
No. 3 " "
1st Field Amb.

1. The transport of 1st Field Ambulance, No. 2 and 3 Companies, Divisional Train and that portion of 143 and 144 Brigades transport which cannot be taken by train (see para. 4), (the whole under Command of Lieut.Col. Crosskey, A.S.C) will march on 29th instant to WORMHOUDT area - Route - NORDAUSQUES - OUEST MONT - WATTEN - LES CLITRES - MERKEGHEM. Starting point - road junction 400 yards N.W. of MONNECOVE on NORDAUSQUES - TILQUES road. Head of column to pass at 9 a.m.

Each formation will send an officer to report to Lieut. Col. Crosskey at the starting point at 8.45 a.m.

2. Billets for night 29/30th will be obtained from Area Commandant, WORMHOUDT to whom advanced parties will report 3 hours before arrival of Column.

3. The March will be continued on 30th instant into 18th Corps area under the orders of Lieut.Col. Crosskey.
Route - HOUTKERQUE - ST. JAN TER BIEZEN. Final destinations will be notified to Lieut.Col. Crosskey.

4. Personnel of (and part 1st line transport) 143 and 144 Brigades, and personnel 1st Field Ambulance move by rail from AUDRUICQ on 30th instant.
Detraining stations - VLAMERTINGHE for personnel - PESELHOEK for transport.
Each Brigade group will have two tactical and two Omnibus trains. The 1st Field Ambulance will travel with 143 Brigade group.
For composition of Tactical and Omnibus Trains see S.S. 200, page 11.12.
All transport not shown in tables B and C page 11.12 S.S. 200 as being taken in the Omnibus Trains will proceed by road on the 29th instant (see para. 1).

5. Times of departure of trains will be wired to Brigades as soon as known. Personnel must be at the station 1 hour and transport 3 hours before departure of train.
Each Brigade group will detail a fatigue party of 100 men under an officer for loading at entraining station and another party of 100 for unloading at PESELHOEK.

6. All troops proceeding by rail on 30th instant will take rations for consumption 30th and 31st. O.C. Train will arrange to deliver these by evening of 29th.

7. From 8 a.m. on 28th Brigadier-General DONE, D.S.O., Commanding 144 Inf.Bde. will be in command of troops in rear area. He will issue necessary instructions to 143 Brigade and 1st Field Ambulance as to times of trains and march to AUDRUICQ.
He will also detail an officer as assistant to the R.T.O. at both entraining and detraining stations.

6

P.T.O.

Capt. Gibson will remain at CHATEAU COCOVE until 30th instant and will act as liaison officer between Traffic, HAZEBROUCK - 19th Corps and Brigadier-General DONE, informing the latter of any orders received re trains and movements. He will also deal with any demands for extra lorries.

8. Acknowledge.

Issued at p.m.

Lieut.Colonel,
A.A. & Q.M.G., 48th Division.

Copy No. 1. 19th Corps
" " 2. 18th Corps
" " 3. Brig-Genl.Done,D.S.O.
" " 4. 144 Bde.
" " 5. 143 "
" " 6. 1st Fd. Amb.
" " 7. Div. Train.
" " 8. Lt.Col.Crosskey.
" " 9. "G"
" " 10. 58th Division.
" " 11.)
" " 12.) Retained.
" " 13.)

SECRET. Copy No. . . .

143rd Inf. Bde. OPERATION ORDER NO.107.

Ref. map
1/100,000 HAZEBROUCK 5A.

28th Sept.,1917.

1. The Bde. will move to DAMBRE CAMP, XVIII Corps area, on Sunday 30 th Sept.

2. Part of the transport will proceed by road under Lieut. USHER, 5th R.War.R. under orders already issued.

3. The Bde.(less transport referred to in para 2) will entrain at AUDRUICQ in accordance with entraining table attached.

4. Troops entraining on personnel train will arrive at entraining station 1 hour before their train is due to depart.
Troops entraining on omnibus train will arrive at entraining station 3 hours before their train is due to depart.
5th R.War.R. to be clear of NORDAUSQUES 3½ hours before time of departure of train.
8th R.War.R. will not cross the CALAIS-ST OMER Road before the 5th Bn. is clear.

5. Trains at the disposal of the Bde. will be :-

2 tactical trains (44 3rd Class coaches)
2 omnibus trains (1 coach, 17 flats and 30 covered vans.)

6. The following parties will be found :-

5th R.War.R. - 1 Officer and 50 O.R. (entraining party) to report to R.T.O. at AUDRUICQ 3 hours before the time of the 1st Omnibus train.
8th R.War.R. - 1 Officer and 50 O.R. (detraining party) to travel by the 1st Omnibus train and to report to the R.T.O. at PESELHOEK on arrival.

7. An Officer of the Bde. Staff will be at AUDRUICQ to assist the R.T.O. until the whole Bde. is entrained.
Lieut. WALKER, Bde. Staff, will report to R.T.O. VLAMERTINGHE as detraining Officer.

8. An advance party of 1 Officer and 5 N.C.O.s per Bn. 1 Officer and 1 N.C.O. from M.G.Coy. and 1 N.C.O. from T.M.Batt. will proceed by the 1st personnel train and will report to Lieut. WALKER at the detraining station.

9. Lorries will be allotted as follows :-
1 lorry for the 6th and 8th Bn. R.War.R.
1 ,, ,, ,, 5th and 7th Bn. ,,
1 ,, ,, ,, M.G.Coy. and T.M.Batt.
1 ,, ,, ,, Bde. Hdqrs.
These will report to 6th R.War.R., 7th R.War.R., T.M.Batt. and Bde. Hdqrs. respectively on the evening of the 29th inst and will proceed by road to DAMBRE CAMP.
They will be found from 48th Div. Supply Column.
Other lorries will be available to take kits and packs to entraining station, further details later.

10. An Officer from each unit will report to Staff Capt. at AUDRUICQ 1½ hours before their train is due to leave and he will hand to the R.T.O. an entraining state for his unit. A copy of this state will also be sent to Bde. Hdqrs. by 6 p.m. on 29th inst.

11. Rations will be carried by units for the 30th Sept. and 1st Oct. These will be delivered by the evening of 29th inst.

12. ACKNOWLEDGE.

Captain,
B.M. 143rd Inf. Bde.

Issued at

Entraining Table issued with 143rd Inf. Bde. O.O. 187

SERIAL NO.	UNIT	NO. OF TRAIN	STATION	TRAIN ARRIVE	TRAIN DEPART	DESTINATION	REMAKRS
1	5th R. War.R. 8th R.War.R. (less entraining and detraining parties) T.M.Batt. M.G.Coy. Adv. parties from all units.	1	AUDRUICQ	Times will be notified later.		VLAMERTINGHT	
2.	Bde. Hdqrs. 6th Bn. R.War.R. 7th Bn. R.War.R. 1st Fd. Amb.	2.	,,	,,		,,	
3.	Transport of serial No. 1 Detraining party of 8th R.War.R.	1A	,,	,,		PESELHOEK	The R.T.O. will be in charge of the detraining at PESELHOEK
4.	Transport of serial No. 2 Entraining party of 5th R.War.R.	2A	,,	,,		,,	,,

Omnibus train consists of 30 covered vans, 17 flats and 1 coach (to hold 40)
Personnel train ,, ,, 44 coaches (each to hold 40)

Probable duration of journey - 4 hours.

S E C R E T.

Copy No. 11

ADDENDUM NO.1 to 143rd Infantry Brigade OPERATION ORDER NO.167.

29th September, 1917.

1. Times of arrival and departure of Trains are as follows :-

SERIAL NO.	TRAIN ARRIVE	TRAIN DEPART.
1	5 a.m.	6 a.m.
2	9 a.m.	10 a.m.
3	6 a.m.	9 a.m.
4	12 noon.	3 p.m.

2. ACKNOWLEDGE.

[signature]

Captain,
B.M. 143rd Inf. Bde.

Issued at 9.30 a.m.

Copies to all recipients of
143rd Inf.Bde. O.O.167.

140/2499.

1st South Midland F. A.

11

WAR DIARY

or

INTELLIGENCE SUMMARY.

(Erase heading not required.)

Army Form C. 2118.

Vol 31

Instructions regarding War Diaries and Intelligence Summaries are contained in F. S. Regs., Part II. and the Staff Manual respectively. Title pages will be prepared in manuscript.

Place	Date	Hour	Summary of Events and Information	Remarks and references to Appendices
			War Diary	
			1/1st South Midland Field Amb^ce	
			1st October 1917 to 31 October 1917	

D. D. & L., London, E.C.
(A7883) Wt. W803/M1672 350,000 4/17 Sch. 52a Forms/C/2118/14

Instructions regarding War Diaries and Intelligence Summaries are contained in F. S. Regs., Part II. and the Staff Manual respectively. Title pages will be prepared in manuscript.

WAR DIARY
or
~~INTELLIGENCE SUMMARY.~~
(Erase heading not required.)

Army Form C. 2118.

Place	Date	Hour	Summary of Events and Information	Remarks and references to Appendices
L'ABBE FARM	1.10.17		9.0 am. Parade Inspection by Commanding Officer.	
			Awaiting orders. 12 noon. Received order to proceed	
			to Cwent Farm. 2.30 pm. Unit proceeded by Dranoutre	
			Route & arrived at Cwent Farm at 3 pm. Awaiting	
			orders. "B" Section Tent Sub. Div. returned from 32 C.C.Stn	
CWENT FARM	2.10.17		9.0 am Parade Inspection by Commanding Officer —	
			Respirator Drill. A party of Seventy other	
			ranks proceeded to Advanced Dressing Station	
			Dunallow for duty with 1/3rd S. Mid. Field Amb.	
CWENT FARM	3.10.17		6.0 am. Reveille. 6.30 am Parade. All Billets cleaned	
			out. 7.30 am Breakfast. 9.0 am. Parade Fighting	
			Order & proceeded to take over Advanced Dressing	
			Station Dunallow. "A" & "B" Tent Sub. Divisions	
			relieved two Tent Sub Divisions of 1/3rd South	
			Midland Field Ambulance already doing duty	
			at A.D.S. Dunallow. Relief completed by	

D. D. & L., London, E.C. (A7883) Wt. W803/M1672 350,000 4/17 Sch. 52a Forms/C/2118/14

Instructions regarding War Diaries and Intelligence Summaries are contained in F. S. Regs., Part II. and the Staff Manual respectively. Title pages will be prepared in manuscript.

WAR DIARY
or
~~INTELLIGENCE SUMMARY.~~
(Erase heading not required.)

Army Form C. 2118.

Place	Date	Hour	Summary of Events and Information	Remarks and references to Appendices
	3.10.17	–	12 noon – The three Bearer Sub Divisions were attached for duty to O.Comdg 1/2nd South Midland Field Ambulance who was in charge of the evacuations from the Regimental Aid Posts to Advanced Dressing Station DUHALLOW. Copy of 48 Division R.A.M.C. Operation Order No 7 of 3.10.17 attached hereto, which will show the scheme of evacuation carried out	
A.D.S. Duhallow	2.10.17 10.10.17		During this period the Unit was in charge of the Advanced Dressing Station Duhallow. The following casualties were dealt with during 2.10.17 to 11.10.17.	
			48th Division	
			Officers. — Lying 25; Sitting 10; Total 35	
			Other Ranks. — Lying 374; Sitting 188; Walking 466; Total 1028	

D. D. & L., London, E.C. (A7883) Wt. W803/M1672 350,000 4/17 Sch. 52a Forms/C/2118/14

Instructions regarding War Diaries and Intelligence Summaries are contained in F. S. Regs., Part II. and the Staff Manual respectively. Title pages will be prepared in manuscript.

WAR DIARY
or
~~INTELLIGENCE~~ SUMMARY.
(Erase heading not required.)

Army Form C. 2118.

Place	Date	Hour	Summary of Events and Information	Remarks and references to Appendices
A.D.S. Duhallow	2.10.17 to 10.10.17	–	48th Division Continued	
			Deaths – Officers 2. Other Ranks 4	
			Other Formations.	
			Officers. Other Ranks.	
			Lying 18 Lying 188	
			Sitting 23 Sitting 380	
			Total 41. Total 568.	
			Deaths.	
			Officers. 2. Other Ranks 4	
			German Prisoners of War.	
			Lying 44. Sitting 57. Deaths 1.	

D. D. & L., London, E.C.
(A7883) Wt. W803/M1672 350,000 4/17 Sch. 52a. Forms/C/2118/14

Instructions regarding War Diaries and Intelligence Summaries are contained in F. S. Regs., Part II. and the Staff Manual respectively. Title pages will be prepared in manuscript.

WAR DIARY
or
~~INTELLIGENCE SUMMARY.~~

(Erase heading not required.)

Army Form C. 2118.

Place	Date	Hour	Summary of Events and Information	Remarks and references to Appendices
A.D.S. Duhallow	3.10.17 to 10.10.17		Special Cases All Formations Officers + Other Ranks.	
			Chest wounds 73 – Head Wounds 49 Abdominal 31	
			Compound Fracture Femur 20.	
			Total Cases dealt with 1773.	
F.D.S. Duhallow	10.10.17		Relief carried out as per Copy of 48th Division R.A.M.C. Operation Order No 10 d/- 9.10.17. Relief Completed by 6 pm. Unit proceeded to School Camp.	
School Camp	11.10.17		Awaiting Orders. Personnel engaged on General fatigues + cleaning their clothing + equipment	
School Camp	12.10.17		6.30 am Reveille 7.0 am Breakfast 9.0 am Parade. Inspection by Commanding Officer Inspection of	

D. D. & L., London, E.C. (A7883) Wt. W803/M1672 350,000 4/17 Sch. 52a Forms/C/2118/14

WAR DIARY
or
~~INTELLIGENCE~~ SUMMARY.
(Erase heading not required.)

Army Form C. 2118.

Instructions regarding War Diaries and Intelligence Summaries are contained in F. S. Regs., Part II. and the Staff Manual respectively. Title pages will be prepared in manuscript.

Place	Date	Hour	Summary of Events and Information	Remarks and references to Appendices
Proven Camp	2.11.17		Equipment & Clothing by Quartermaster. General Fatigues. 2 pm Parade. Inspection of Respirators & Respirator Drill. Awaiting Orders to move into new Divisional Area. All wagons were loaded & roped down. Received 166th Infantry Brigade Order No 206 Copy No 12 d. 2.11.17 copy attached hereto, with reference to the move from Fifth Army Area to First Army Area. "A" Section Tent Sub Division rejoined Unit from No 12 Casualty Clearing Station.	
Proven Camp	3.11.17		6.0 am Reveille. 7.30 am Breakfast. 9.0 am Parade. General Fatigues. 12.30 am Dinner. 2.15 pm Parade. Full Marching Order. Steel Helmets to be worn. Unit proceeded by Road route to Entraining Station at HEDOUTRE	
LIGNY ST FLOCHEL	4.11.17		Detrained at LIGNY ST FLOCHEL at 6 am & proceeded	

D. D. & L., London, E.C. (A7883) Wt. W803/M1672 350,000 4/17 Sch. 52a Forms C/2118/14

Instructions regarding War Diaries and Intelligence Summaries are contained in F. S. Regs., Part II, and the Staff Manual respectively. Title pages will be prepared in manuscript.

WAR DIARY
or
~~INTELLIGENCE~~ SUMMARY.
(Erase heading not required.)

Army Form C. 2118.

Place	Date	Hour	Summary of Events and Information	Remarks and references to Appendices
LIGNY St FLOCHEL	14.10.17		by March Route to VILLERS St. SIMON arriving at 9.30 am. Personnel resting. Awaiting Orders. Received A.D.M.S. operation Order No 11 of 14.10.17 copy attached hereto	
VILLERS. St. SIMON	15.10.17.		6.0 am. Reveille. 6.30 am. Parade. General Fatigues 7.0 am. Breakfast 9.0 am. Parade full Marching Order. Unit proceeded by March Route to FRESNICOURT arrived at FRESNICOURT at 2 pm. Awaiting to take over V Corps Rest Station from 2nd Canadian Division.	
FRESNICOURT	16.10.17. to 21.10.17.		During this period the Unit was waiting to take over V Corps Rest Station from the 2nd Canadian Division. General Fatigues & Route Marches were carried out.	
FRESNICOURT	22.10.17		Relieved the 2nd Canadian Field Ambulance & took over V. Corps Rest Station.	

D. D. & L., London, E.C.
(A7883) Wt. W809/M1672 350,000 4/17 Sch. 52a Forms/C/2118/14

Instructions regarding War Diaries and Intelligence Summaries are contained in F. S. Regs., Part II. and the Staff Manual respectively. Title pages will be prepared in manuscript.

WAR DIARY
or
~~INTELLIGENCE SUMMARY.~~
(Erase heading not required.)

Army Form C. 2118.

Place	Date	Hour	Summary of Events and Information	Remarks and references to Appendices
FRESNICOURT	22.10.17		The following is a description of the accommodation	
			13 French Huts each 100 x 22 ft. Eleven of these being used as Wards & one fitted up for & used by ^last^ Sisters. The remaining one is used as billet for personnel. Each Hut accommodates 50 patients. Total accommodation Sisters 25 Other Ranks ~~[illegible]~~ 650.	
			1 French Hut 27 x 22 ft used as Pack store and Hospital Office	
			1 French Hut 40 x 22 ft used as Quartermaster Stores	
			1 French Hut 25 x 22 ft used as Dressing Room	
			1 Hut 20 x 12 ft used as Fumigator	
			1 Hut 27 x 19½ ft used as Operating Room & Baths	
			The Chateau ~~accommodation~~ was utilised as	

D. D. & L., London, E.C. (A7883) Wt. W803/M1672 350,000 4/17 Sch. 52a Forms/C/2118/14

Instructions regarding War Diaries and Intelligence Summaries are contained in F. S. Regs., Part II. and the Staff Manual respectively. Title pages will be prepared in manuscript.

WAR DIARY
or
~~INTELLIGENCE~~ SUMMARY.
(Erase heading not required.)

Army Form C. 2118.

Place	Date	Hour	Summary of Events and Information	Remarks and references to Appendices
FRESNICOURT	23.10.17		Wards for Sick Officers. Out Officers Cook-house + Stores. The total accommodation being Officers: 9.	
FRESNICOURT	24.10.17		6.0 am Reveille 7.15 am Breakfast 7.25 am Parade for Hospital Day Staff. 8.15 am. Parade for C.D. Section. General Fatigues. 12.30 pm. Dismissal. 1.45 pm Parade for C.D. Section. 4.30 pm. Dismissal. 7.25 pm Parade for Hospital Night Staff.	
FRESNICOURT	24.10.17 – 30.10.17		During this period general fatigues were carried out cleaning up the Huts + Officers Quarters + generally making improvements on the existing accommodation. A room was utilised in the village by Capt W Coates as Dental Mechanics Workshop where minor repairs were attended to. The total Number of Patients in the Rest Station is Officers 4 Other Ranks 463. The prevailing	

D. D. & L., London, E.C. (A7883) Wt. W803/M1672 350,000 4/17 Sch. 52a Forms/C/2118/14

Instructions regarding War Diaries and Intelligence Summaries are contained in F. S. Regs., Part II, and the Staff Manual respectively. Title pages will be prepared in manuscript.

WAR DIARY
or
~~INTELLIGENCE SUMMARY.~~
(Erase heading not required.)

Army Form C. 2118.

Place	Date	Hour	Summary of Events and Information	Remarks and references to Appendices
FRESNICOURT	20.10.17 to 31.10.17		Diseases [illegible] + P.U.O.	
			The following Officers N.C.O.s + Men have been struck off the strength of the Unit during the past month for the reasons stated against their names:-	

Unit.	Reg. No.	Rk.	Name.	Remarks	Date	Wounded &c.
1/1st [illegible] Cumberland	235200	Pte	Smith J. C.	to C.C.S.	2.10.17	Sick
— do —	235258	"	McCormack J. G.	— do —	2.10.17	Sick
— do —	235277	"	Allen G. A.	— do —	2.10.17	Sick
— do —	235197	"	Bullock H.	— do —	6.10.17	Wounded
[illegible] attached	2/4 208685	L/Cpl.	Jones D. A.	— do —	8.10.17	do
— do —	2/4 208671	Do	Baker A. E.	— do —	8.10.17	do
— do —	2/4 208679	"	Clough R.	— do —	8.10.17	do
— do —	2/4 252246	"	Pope E.	— do —	8.10.17	do.
— do —	2/4 208686	"	Broadway C.	— do —	8.10.17	do
— do —	2/4 208678	"	Whittingham C.	— do —	8.10.17	do.
1/5th Manchester attached	252224	"	Worrall	— do —	8.10.17	do.

D. D. & L., London, E.C. (A7883) Wt. W803/M1672 350,000 4/17 Sch. 52a Forms/C/2118/14

Instructions regarding War Diaries and Intelligence Summaries are contained in F. S. Regs., Part II, and the Staff Manual respectively. Title pages will be prepared in manuscript.

WAR DIARY

or

~~INTELLIGENCE SUMMARY.~~

(Erase heading not required.)

Army Form C. 2118.

Place	Date	Hour	Summary of Events and Information	Remarks and references to Appendices
			1/5th Manchester attached 400521 Pte Foley C.C.S. 8.10.17	Wounded.
			1/1st E. Lancs Field Amb. 425524 " Mawby C.C.S. 12.10.17	Gassed.
			— do — — Lieut Davison L. L. 2nd Reserve 18.10.17	Permanent Duty
			— do — 388255 L/Cpl. Purdy Park C.C.S. 20.10.17	Sick
			— do — 392148. Pte Sowley — " — 20.10.17	Sick.
			— do — 425509 " Palmer E. Granville Railway 26.10.17	Permanent Duty
			— do — 425514 " Davey A. E. Country Gran. 1/3rd E. Lancs Amb. 30.10.17	— do —
			The following man has been taken on the Strength of the Unit during the month.	
			R.A.M.C. Pte Wilton from Granville Railway Country Gran. 29.10.17	Permanent Duty
			The following men have been awarded the Military Medal: 425523 Pte Oakeshaw C.W. } 425169 " Rowland W. } Authority XVIII Corps. No. D/ 23/267 + 48th Div. A.R./185	

[signature]

SECRET.

48th.Division R.A.M.C. OPERATION ORDER No 7, by
Colonel R. PICKARD, C.M.G., A.M.S.
A.D.M.S., 48th. Division.

3rd.October 1917.

Ref. Map Sheet BELGIUM 28 N.W.2
1/10,000.

1. The Division will attack on its present front on a day and hour to be given later.

2. The following Medical Posts will be established-

			R.A.M.C. Officers	R.A.M.C. Bearers
REGTL. AID POSTS.	Left, MON DU HIBOU,	C.6.c.2.3.	-	40
	Right, JANET FARM,	C.12.d.5.3.	-	40
RELAY POSTS.	ST. JULIEN	C.12.c.4.6.	-	20
		C.18.a.1.7.	1	20
	VANHEULE FARM	C.17.d.2.6.	1	20
	TIN HUT	C.23.a.4.2.	-	20
DIVISIONAL COLLECTING POST.	CALIFORNIA TRENCH,	C.22.b.7.1.		Half tent Subdvn. 20 bearers.
BEARER POSTS. (local casualties)	CANOPUS TRENCH	C.17.a.4.6.		8 "
	ADMIRALS CROSS ROADS	C.22.c.5.5.		8 "
	LA BELLE ALLIANCE	C.20.d.4.3.		Reserve Bearers.
ADVANCED DRESSING STATION.	DUHALLOW	C.25.d.3.0.		2 Tent Subdivns.

3. EVACUATION OF WOUNDED.

(a) Lying & Sitting:- By car from Relay Post (C.18.a.1.7.) ST. JULIEN, to Divisional Collecting Post, and thence by rail or car to Advanced Dressing Station, DUHALLOW, thence to Casualty Clearing Station or Corps Main Dressing Station by No.24 Motor Ambulance Cars.
10 Motor Ambulance Convoy cars will be allotted for working between the Divisional Collecting Post and Advanced Dressing Station.

(b) Walking: On foot to Divisional Collecting Post, CALIFORNIA TRENCH, then by rail or on foot to Advanced Dressing Station. From Advanced Dressing Station by lorries to Corps Walking Wounded Collecting Post.

(c) Cases other than those East of STEENBEEK: Will go to nearest Relay Post.

(d) Light Railway: 2 Trains of 3 wagons each will be provided. A spur line terminating near Divisional Collecting Post will be used for loading.
Line is controlled by O.C., No.29 Light Railway Coy. TROIS TOURS.
Orderlies will be provided by O.C. 1/3rd.S.Mid. Field Ambulance.

4. DUTIES OF O.Cs FIELD AMBULANCES.

(a) O.C. 1/3rd. S.M.Field Ambulance will be in charge of the evacuation from Regimental Aid Posts to Advanced Dressing Station.
Personnel, (1) Bearer divisions of 3 Field Ambulances;
(2) 2 Tent Subdivns of 1/3rd.S.Mid. Field Ambulance.

(b) O.C. 1/1st.S.M.Field Ambulance will be in charge of Advanced Dressing Station, DUHALLOW, and passing over of cases to Motor Ambulance Convoy.
Personnel, 2 Tent Sub-divisions of 1/1st.S.Mid. Field Ambulance;

(c) O.C. 1/2nd.S.mid.Field Ambulance will be in charge of a Section at Corps Main Dressing Station.
Personnel, 2 Tent Subdivns, and 7 Nursing Orderlies from 1/3rd.S.Mid. Field Ambulance.
2 Medical Officers 58th.Division.

5. RESERVE INFANTRY BEARERS.

1½ Companies will be detailed.
3 Platoons will report at Advanced Dressing Station on "Y" Day at 5 p.m.
(2 Platoons will be sent to Regimental Aid Post MON DU HIBOU, 1 to Regimental Aid Post JANET FARM.)

3 Platoons will report at Advanced Dressing Station on "Z" Day at 9 a.m. The latter will be at the disposal of A.D.M.S.

6. Attention is drawn to -
(a) 48th.Divisional R.A.M.C. Operation Order No.3, paras. 6, 8, 9 & 10.
(b) 48th. Divisional R.A.M.C. ~~Order~~ Circular Memo No 2 of 31-7-17
(c) D.M.S. Fifth Army Circular Memo. No.41 d/d 1st.Sept.17.

7. All German wounded prisoners will have their documents taken away from them at the Advanced Dressing Station: these will be made up into packets and handed to 48th. Div. Headquarters.

8. ACKNOWLEDGE.

R. PICKARD. Colonel,

A.D.M.S., 48th.Division.

SECRET.

48th. Division, Operation Order No. 9.

by Colonel R.Pickard, C.M.G., A.M.S.

7th. Oct. 1917.

Ref. Map Sheet BELGIUM 28 N.W.2, 1/10,000.

1. The Division will attack on its present front on a day and hour to be given later.

2. The following will be the Medical Posts for the operations,

			Off.	Bearers.
REGIMENTAL AID POSTS.	Right, JANET,	C.12.d.5.5.	-	40.
	Left, Hubner,	D.1.c.4.6.	-	40.
R.A.M.C. RELAY POSTS.	MON DU HIBOU,	C.6.c.2.3.		
	TRIANGLE.	C.6.c.7.2.		20.
	ST. JULIEN.	C.12.c.4.6.		40.
Divl. COLLECTING POST.	ST. JULIEN.	C.18.a.1.7.	½ Tent Sub-Divn. 40 Bearers.	
RESERVE BEARER POSTS.	VANHEULE	C.17.d.2.9.	½ Tent Sub-Divn.	
	CALIFORNIS.	C.22.b.7.1.	10 Bearers.	
	LA BELLE ALLIANCE.	C.20.d.3.0.	Reserve.	
ADVANCED DRESSING STATION.	DUHALLOW.	C.25.d.3.0.	3 Tent Sub-Divisions.	

3. EVACUATIONS will be by hand and wheeled stretcher to Divl. Collecting Post, thence by cars or rail from C.17.b.8.9. to Advanced Dressing Station.

4. RESERVE INFANTRY BEARERS, Three Platoons will be available on Y day, 1 will be used in front of JANET, 2 in front of HUBNER.

5. DUTIES of Os.C. Field Ambulances.
As in R.A.M.C.Operation Order No. 7 d/d 3-10-17.

6. ACKNOWLEDGE.

(Signed) R.Pickard, Colonel,

A.D.M.S., 48th. Division.

SECRET. 4ith. Division, R.A.M.C. Operation Order No. 10.

9th. Oct. 1917.

Ref. Map Sheets 28 & 27.

1. The Division will be relieved in the line by the 9th. Division on the night 10/11th. Oct. 1917.

2. (a) The 1/1st. South Midland Field Ambulance will pass over the Advanced Dressing Station, DUHALLOW, to the incoming Field Ambulance of the 9th. Division on the 10th. inst. It will move to SCHOOL CAMP.

(b) 1/3rd. South Midland Field Ambulance will hand over R.A.M.C. posts in the area East of the Canal to the incoming Field Ambulance of the 9th. Division. It will move to L'EBBE FARM.

(c) The 2 Tent sub-divisions of the 1/2nd.S.Mid.Field Ambulance will be relieved at Corps Main Dressing Station by a Tent sub-division of the 9th.Division. Their Tent Sub-division at the Corps Walking Wounded Collecting Post will be similarly relieved by a Tent-subdivision of the 9th. Division. They will move to TUNNELLERS Camp.

All these moves to be complete by 6 p.m. on the 10th. inst. In the case of (a) and (b) sufficient personnel will be left behind to deal with the casualties of the 48th. Division still to be collected. Further orders will be given on this point. The Officers and personnel of the 58th. Division will be passed over to the 9th. Division.

In handing over material strict accuracy must be exercised, and greatcare taken that no material is left in the field.

3. SICK. The Field Ambulances will collect the sick in their new camps.

4. A.D.M.S. Office is situate at X Camp A.16.c .2.4.

5. ACKNOWLEDGE.

R.Pickard, Colonel,

A.D.M.S. 48th. Division.

48th. Division , R.A.M.C. ORDER No. 192.

by COLONEL R. PICKARD, C.M.G., A.M.S.

11th. Oct., 1917.

1. For the purposes of the forthcoming move the Field Ambulances of the Division will be affiliated as follows :-
   1/1st.S.M.Fd.Ambce. to 144th.Inf. Bde.
   1/2nd.S.M.Fd.Ambce. to 145th.Inf. Bde.
   1/3rd.S.M.Fd.Ambce. to 143rd.Inf. Bde.
   Orders will be issued to the Field Ambulances by the Brigades concerned.

2. Each Field Ambulance will be responsible for the collection of sick of its Brigade during the move and on arrival in the new area.

3. A.D.M.S. Office in "X" Camp will close on 13th. inst. at noon, and reopen at the same day and hour at a place to be notified later.

4. ACKNOWLEDGE.

R.Pickard, Colonel,

A.D.M.S., 48th. Division.

SECRET.

R.A.M.C. 48th.Division OPERATION ORDER No 11, 14th.Oct.1917.

1. The 48th. Division will relieve the 2nd.Canadian Division in the line.

2. MOVES AND DUTIES OF FIELD AMBULANCES.

(a) 1/1st.S.Mid.Field Ambulance will move to FRESNICOURT on the 15th. Inst. It will take over the duties of the Corps Rest Station when the Field Ambulance of the Canadian Division move out.

(b) The 1/2nd.S.Mid.Field Ambulance will send an advance party on the 15th. inst to the 5th. Canadian Field Ambulance at MONT ST ELOI to learn the method of clearing from the line, and to take over the posts and material. The main party will move to MONT ST ELOI and will take over the collection of sick and wounded from the line, to be completed by Noon on 17th. inst.

(c) The 1/3rd.S.Mid. Field Ambulance will send an advance party on 15th.inst. to take over :-

(1) Field Ambulance encampment at CHATEAU DE LA HAIE;
(2) Medical Detention Room and encampment at VILLERS AU BOIS.
(3) Field Ambulance encampment at QUATRE VENTS.;
(4) Corps Infectious Hospital at ESTREE CAUCHIE.

On the 16th. inst. the main party will move to,-

(1) CHATEAU DE LA HAIE - Headquarters.
(2) VILLERS AU BOIS - 1 Tent subdivision.
(3) QUATRE VENTS- 1 N.C.O. & 4 men.
(4) ESTREE CAUCHIE - 1 Tent subdivision.

3. ACKNOWLEDGE.

R.PICKARD, Colonel,
A.D.M.S., 48th. Division.

SECRET.

No. 103.

48th. Division MEDICAL ARRANGEMENTS.

1. Posts as follows :- Ref.Map Sheet LENS 1/100,000.
" 36c S.W. 1/20,000.

Regimental Aid Posts, Right, T.16.c.5.9. Junction of TEDDY GERARD & TORONTO RD.
Left, T.15.a.6.6. PEGGIE TRENCH.
T.8.c.9.6. Hayter Trench.
Relay Post, T.8.a.5.7. Head of Light Railway.

Divisional Collecting Post. T.22.c.6.4.
T.25.a.9.4. VIMY.
S.18.c.9.6. BOIS DE CHAUDIERE.
Advanced Dressing Stations, NEUVILLE ST VAAST
AUX RIETZ.

Medical Detention Rooms, CHATEAU DE LA HAIE.
VILLERS AU BOIS.
Corps Rest Station, (including Scabies) FRESNICOURT
Corps Infectious Diseases Hospital, ESTREE CAUCHIE.
Casualty Clearing Statios, BRUAY, BARLIN.

2. 1/2nd.S.M.Field Ambulance will collect sick and wounded from the front line.
1/3rd.S.M.Field Ambulance will collect sick from the remaining portion of the Divisional area, establishing Detention Huts at VILLERS AU BOIS and CHATEAU DE LA HAIE, in addition to staffing Corps Infectious Hospital at Estree Cauchie.

3. (1) Cases likely to recover in 48 hours will be detained at the 1/3rd.S.M.Field Ambulance.
(2) Cases likely to be well in over 2 days and under 14 days will be sent to Corps Rest Station.
(3) Caes likely to exceed 14 days will be sent to Casualty Clearing Station at BRUAY or BARLIN.

4. Instructions regarding Infectious cases and other special cases will be issued later.

14-10-17

R.Pickard, Colonel,
A.D.M.S., 48th. Division.

www.ingramcontent.com/pod-product-compliance
Lightning Source LLC
Chambersburg PA
CBHW080846230426
43662CB00013B/2035